Gaslight

Books by Carol Guess
Gaslight
Seeing Dell
Switch

Gaslight

by Carol Guess

Odd Girls Press ✧ Anaheim, CA

First edition, 2001
10 9 8 7 6 5 4 3 2 1

Library of Congress
Cataloging-in-Publication Data   2001094565 CIP

Guess, Carol
Gaslight / Carol Guess
p. 192 cm.
ISBN (trade paper): 1-887237-05-4

Anorexia nervosa — Patients Biography.
Anorexia nervosa — Social aspects.
Authorship — Sex differences.
Autobiography.
Autobiography — Women authors.
Creative writing (Higher education) — Social aspects.
English language — Rhetoric — Study and teaching
      — Social aspects.
Women authors — Biography.
Women — Education (Higher) — Feminism and education.

Gaslight is dedicated to Sandy Yannone

Fat Rosie and Rose is dedicated to
Deborah Archer

Acknowledgments

Portions of this manuscript first appeared in *Fourth Genre, Harrington Lesbian Fiction Quarterly,* and *The Harvard Gay and Lesbian Review* in slightly different form.

Thanks to Brandon Derfler, Esther Eppele, Jackie Fiegel, Gigi Grinstad, Carolyn Koehnline, Laura Laffrado, Bill Lyne, Rosanne Kanhai, Sarah Madsen, Tonia Matthew, Sarah McCarry, Serene Petersen, Donna Qualley, Marian Rodriguez, and Kathryn Stevenson for encouragement, and to K. Flaherty Maddox Regan and Nichola Torbett for friendship across the miles. I'm indebted to Deborah Archer, Eric Wendt, Sandy Yannone, and several anonymous reviewers for comments on early drafts of this manuscript.

Thanks to Margaret Gillon at Odd Girls Press for taking a risk on my writing, and insisting that feminist publishing remains viable and vital. Inky thanks to my editor, Katherine V. Forrest, whose own writing moved me long before her intelligent edits helped me craft the final version of this book.

Thanks to Debra Salazar for bringing me back to shore.

Special thanks to my family, Alison, Gerry, and Harry Guess, whose love, patience, and creativity continue to guide me.

Daddy says I got my mama's mouth
I'm all about
a forked tongue and a dirty house

        Sleater-Kinney, *Youth Decay*

Now as you turn, now as you traipse with combat boots and negligee into that good night. Away. But turn, for one brief second, back.

        Carole Maso, *Aureole*

Contents

One Writer's Ghosts

"You want to make me a ghost," she said, looking away from me to sunlight spilled like white wine on dark wood. And later, "You want to make me a ghost," I echoed, as she snapped a photograph of my face lit by a candle, gold sheen on my pale hair.

Sometimes everything comes together in a single instant, a single color, a flash of light like a snapshot. Pain and pleasure, detours and desire, past and present merge as ghost selves become visible to the bodies they've haunted. My thirtieth year was like that: glint, my vision blurring between *now* and *never, flee* and *forever.* My thirtieth year marks a milestone in a life marred by amnesia and melancholia, marks the end of one self and the start of another — Kate to Callie to Cassie to who?

"It takes so long," she wrote of our writing, our conversations, our lovemaking. I am writing these words for a particular woman, but also for my old selves, and in homage to new ones. It takes so long to remember. To haunt and to be haunted. It takes so long to be re-born.

Not long after turning thirty, early in 1998, I finished my fourth novel, *Retrieval*, and began a fifth. Called *Fat Rosie and Rose*, the book focused on a pregnant teenager. I imagined it as an experiment, not only in content (more overtly political than is usual in my work), but in form. The various voices developed through rhyme and puns, abrupt paragraph breaks and repetition. I wanted *Fat Rosie and Rose* to have scars; I wanted the pages to demonstrate Rose's mindset, but also the state I was in when I began it. I did not want to make it nice and clean and smooth, but to bear witness to the schizophrenic feeling of living in a culture that alternately threatens and denies the existence of sexual women. It seems to me that the damage women suffer in our culture is the same as madness, but the opposite of art. *Fat Rosie* remains my testament to this, precisely because I could not finish it. It does not exist except here, in fragments; it is the fifth novel that now is not and yet will never not be. Like an anoretic's impossible ideal of thinness, like a love triangle's refusal to become a circle, the book refused to become a novel; it remains unrealized, a glinting mirage.

In its place I constructed this text, begun merely as an explanation, the preface to a novel that metamorphosed into memoir. That memoir, *Gaslight*, in turn blurred back into fiction and finally into a palimpsest of a text that demanded the construction of a fictitious self, a narrator who is neither me nor not me, neither wholly intimate nor wholly other. I could tag my lies and truths so that you could follow, but there are no maps here, only motion. This book is homage to my past, to my surviving madness and self-destruction. It is also homage to a lie most writers tell: belief in a theoretical audience, in their trust, interest, confidence.

I took my title from Adrienne Rich's essay "Women and Honor: Some Notes on Lying." Of the lies patriarchal ideologies impose on women, Rich writes, "Women have been driven mad, 'gaslighted,' for centuries by the refutation of our experience and our instincts in a culture which validates only male experience . . . We therefore have a primary obligation . . . not to undermine each other's sense of reality." In *Gaslight* I set out to tell truths I had kept secret from others and even myself; also to examine my own relation to lying as a writer, teacher, daughter, and lover. While I was writing I juxtaposed Rich's essay with Rebecca Brown's brilliant novel *The Terrible Girls*, in which the narrator must come to terms with the lies her lesbian lover tells her, lies which literally cause her body to come undone.

Brown's lyrical gothic aesthetic seemed linked politically, culturally, and geographically to the riot grrrl music scene of the Pacific Northwest, especially to the band Sleater-Kinney, who in their most recent CD lament the appropriation of third-wave feminist culture by capitalist cynics: "But they took our ideas to their marketing stars / And now I'm spending all my days at girlpower.com / Trying to buy back a little piece of me." I saw connections between my own unraveling, Rich's expose of the roots of women's "madness," Brown's passionate, wounded narrator, and Sleater-Kinney's performative critiques of consumerism and male violence. Yet these links were primarily about content, not form. Finally, while writing *Blue* I discovered Carole Maso's poetic novel *Aureole* (and much later, *The American Woman in the Chinese Hat*, which haunts me still). At last I had found a text whose structure might provide a model. *Aureole* showed me how to link the fragments of *Fat Rosie* with the prose of my preface. Today all of these women's voices swirl around me, guiding me, as I flatter myself that I occasionally inspire my students, who trust me every quarter with smart, startling, original writing.

This book is a graveyard and carnival ride, funeral and wedding. As of this writing there can be no legal marriage between woman and woman. Can I hope for a commitment between reader and writer? Or will you enter *Gaslight* as I once entered my own history — as an outsider, unable to have and to hold?

This book itself is outside itself. Portions are autobi-ography, portions are fiction. Portions are poetry, docu-ment, description. It is a liar's mosaic, as any memoir must be. And body — when I remember my lovers, I let my blood speak. Bodies have their own memories; to inhabit fully a kinesthetic recollection is a kind of ec-stasy, the lilt a saint knows touching a charred or hairy relic.

Feel it. Enter into what I knew, and know — plea-sure, gravity, sorrow. Here are no secrets but this ges-ture: the flick of a wrist turning the pages of a calendar.

Blood

Red

I am fifteen and I have no name, but I am learning how to get into a car without showing my underwear to the men surrounding me.

A woman is teaching me. She has long nails, a short skirt, willowy heels.

"Girls," she says.

There are ten of us in beauty school, ages thirteen to thirty-nine.

"Girls, pretend you are surrounded by handsome men. One of them opens the car door for you. How do you enter?"

I begin by imagining the men in great detail. I give them faces and names because one of them might be my husband. When it's my turn, I totter in my spiky heels to the center of the circle. I sit in the passenger seat, my back to the driver, and swing my legs gracefully, torso twisting in sync.

"Now get out," she says.

And later: *Remember to keep your knees shut tight, like a secret you can't tell.* Her nails are red. One of the men I imagine is real. He has a name and a face and a zippy red car. He is ten years older than me, and a bad driver.

After everyone has had her turn in and out of the car, we leave the parking garage and return to the classroom. One by one we strip to our underwear, step on the scale, and sink. We think about numbers for the first time that week.

When I step on the scale, the women surround me. I feel their stares like heat on my shoulders and thighs. One writes the number in a folder; another tugs on her bra — powder blue. There is so much lace in the room. It makes me happy. At fifteen I like lace and complicated colors — mauve, violet, silver. I like frills and words such as "full-face" and "uplift." They assuage my fears that I do not fit in, fears I cannot name because I cannot point to anything different about me. I look like all the other fifteen-year-olds at my high school: thin, diffident, pastel. We are all anoretic and painfully, almost parodically, feminine. We look like drag queens, except for Jessica, a star on the swim team. She looks like a linebacker.

I avoid her.

My locker is covered with pictures of ballerinas. For reasons I can't explain, I flip through dance magazines, culling pictures of muscular male stars, which I paste carefully over the bodies of Suzanne Farrell, Kyra Nichols, and Heather Watts. When I get to my favorite photo, of Heather Watts twisted into a pretzel, I can't bring myself to cover her with Peter Martins. Instead I leave her, a tiny woman with legs muscled into perfect figure eights, suspended like a question. I also pin up pictures of girls I dance with, their legs twisted into cautious letters. I would like a picture of the man with the red car, but he laughs when I say I want one for my locker.

When he calls, my mother summons me from the bedroom lair where I am sprawled on my futon eating rice cakes and drinking diet soda. She murmurs his name in a studied whisper, but her eyes betray her pleasure. Because I don't have makeup on, I feel self-conscious. I twirl my hair around my finger and shift from foot to foot.

He is a bad driver because I distract him.

At least, this is what he tells me. But when I say *sorry*, he puts his hand on my thigh and twists the steering wheel in an abrupt, deliberate jerk. He was my brother's baby-sitter last summer, while my parents were in Europe and I was at dance camp. My brother liked him, his roguishness, the thick shock of pale hair falling over his left eye. They played good games, my brother says — catch and half-court and Pac Man — and ate McDonald's six nights out of nine. He was a good baby-sitter, my parents agree, and when he calls to ask if I want to go for a walk in Larrett Park one Saturday, I imagine we will play good games, too.

Thirty minutes before he arrives at the house, I am lounging in my bedroom, biting my nails and reading teen magazine articles on bulimia. I am thinking about throwing up, how it would feel, what my mouth would taste like after. In one story a girl eats half a cake and two pints of ice cream before she lets the food slide from her gut to her throat to her lips, then rejects it. I love the articles, love the descriptions before the girl vomits — the decadence of the orgy, the long lists of forbidden foods.

I am daydreaming about ice cream when my mother knocks. She looks startled to find that I am in my nightgown. Her whole face contracts into a clock. "He'll be here in half an hour," she says, folding her hands over and over. They look like water as she waves me into the bathroom. She sits me on the toilet lid and begins to do my face.

When the man with the red car arrives, I am ready. I am wearing a short black skirt safety-pinned around my thinning middle, a long velour black sweater, and a gargantuan pink bow at the back of my head. My bracelets and earrings make a great deal of noise as we walk around the park. Once I burp. I am mortified. He pretends not to hear and when no one is looking, plucks a rare flower and tucks it behind my ear.

In beauty school I am learning about illusion — how to create the simulacrum of depth. When I make up my lips I use a pale, creamy base to destroy their actual shape, so that the face in the classroom mirror has no mouth. Then I outline a new set of lips, whatever shape I please, with brick-red pencil. Next I fill in the outline with movie-star red. For the finale, I smudge a dab of very light pink in line with my nose, at the center of the bow-shape everyone in class is envious of.

Once I emerge with a spectacular Betty Boop smirk that Tara, our Tri-Delta, singles out with the right index finger of her French manicure. "You look twenty-one," she says, her voice a mixture of envy and something else. I don't like the envy, but I like her gesture, which happens in slow motion. I even remember touch, soft soft at my skin, but perhaps I made that up, or make it up now — me, Carol, the storyteller.

The day of our walk in the park, our first time alone, the man with the red car drops me off in time for dinner. I thank him and ask if he'd like to come inside and visit my brother. He is, after all, the baby-sitter.

He cocks his head. His right eye is autumn-amber. "I didn't come for your brother," he says.

After our lessons, after we have created our faces for the week, we put cheesecloth bags over our heads before we tug our smocks off. The bags emerge stained with cheeks, eyes, lips as the pink of our smocks is replaced by cool tans and crisp navys. We learn to fix snags in our hose with nail polish, spreading the sticky stuff over the runs carefully, without concern for the flesh beneath. We learn to fix anything that runs, sags, or bleeds with acrylic and cotton, bobby pins and saccharine.

That long fifteenth year, the year I begin beauty school, the year the man with the red car starts to touch me at night, I hold my breath every week while Glory Sue records my weight. Although I hate the scale's bold proclamations, hate the tears of the girls who have come for this reason, I love the flowers we become when we strip down to our bras and panties. The others wear sophisticated colors — greens, greys, violets that shimmer when they brush past me, biting their lips. We leave our jewelry on, but not our heels; they lie jumbled in a pile like obscure weaponry. Once, as I am tugging my skirt back over my hips, Tara leans towards me, still shirtless, and congratulates me on losing another pound. In the grace of her gesture I see only a shadow, the faint darkness of a line where her cream-colored push-up bra cups meet in a satin bow. My difference is there, in that moment; though I write it off as envy, as wanting to be like Tara, some part of my mind knows it is something else.

In my high school lunchroom, Jessica passes my table carrying a tray filled with food. My friends and I tug the foil tops off plain yogurt, exchange carrot sticks, sip diet soda through bendable straws. When Jessica returns for seconds before Nancy has even finished her symmetrical apple slices, Claire nudges me and I take care of it.

"*Hungry,*" I hiss. The other girls pick it up. *Hungry,* then *Greedy,* then, although Jessica is muscular, a swimmer, *Fatty.*

Fatty becomes *Lezzie.*

And I am safe.

In beauty school I am learning about perspective. One day my teacher, Glory Sue, hands me a bra with breasts already in it. They are flesh-colored, though not the color of my skin, mottled pink and freckled, nor the color of Jasmine's, dark brown with red undertones, but the fragile jaundice-yellow of a sickly baby, whiny and urine-scented, longing for milk. The cloth around the breasts is red — red satin — and Glory Sue winks as she hands it over. When I fold it double, the cups make a hand puppet, red mouth without a voice. Years later, I find it wadded in the back of my dresser and tie it to a doorknob, knowing my cat will show no mercy, knowing that animals, unlike humans, use things in useful ways.

He parks the red car where no one will see its color. He wanted hunter or pewter, something masculine, something stark. Instead there is this red, and me, spread open. I watch the stars through the window when I'm on my back. On my belly, there's nothing to see, so I close my eyes. Once, in the middle of a contortion, he bursts out laughing. When I sit up, frightened, he is holding the red bra.

When he drops me off, the house is dark. In the morning I eat breakfast with my brother, who calls me a slut until our mother shushes him.

At Christmas the parents of the man with the red car give me a necklace — a tiny amber bead encased in gold. They hand me the package, then go into the living room and drink cocktails with my parents. When I show my mother the necklace, she holds it in her palm for a long while. There is something in her eyes; I can't name it. When she gives it back, the amber feels warm.

When the man with the red car comes to our door, my mother checks my makeup and my father hands me money. Every week, excluding holidays, I earn ten dollars because I pocket the cash. It's meant to cover the usual fancies. But the man with the red car pays for everything, so I think of my time with him as free.

He enters. My parents welcome him. Often he sits on the sofa for several minutes, joshing about stock options, baseball, films. He is serious and pseudo-intellectual, which suits his startling eyes and golden hair. He lives with his parents because he is struggling to open his own law business — at twenty-five, no less! *Wunderkind,* my parents joke when they think I can't hear them. They both kiss my forehead before I leave the house. They don't wait up, but they show their concern for our safety — his as well as mine — in the bend that signals *kiss.* Then my father opens the door and everyone watches as I leave the house first. Once, when I turn back, the man with the red car is standing between my parents, the longed-for son of their senior years.

He opens the car door for me. I totter in my spiky heels to the car's gaping red mouth. I sit in the passenger seat, my back to the driver, and swing my legs gracefully, torso twisting in sync.

"Now get out," he says later. We are parked in a deserted lot. The railway station shimmers, ghostly; I will remember its faint outlines better than his hands. I will remember the ghostly silhouettes of buildings, benches, tracks, and the whistle of the trains that pass by but don't stop. Years later, when I see steamed-up cars, I will wonder if the girl waited for her date to open her door and help her out, then into the backseat; if the seat belts left bruises; if the radio was on.

Sometimes he says my name.

At first I don't understand that the moment of naming precedes expulsion. I think that my name, shifting between his lips, is a gift, a moment of identification. But the name is a release, a rush of air that parallels the rush his body makes, all strength and density. No part of me admires it; there is nothing beautiful in it, though years later I will love a man and try to understand what he calls *pleasure*. But for now there is only the dark triangle his body makes, hovering, and his words, sounds really, letters chosen not for meaning but for motion.

Sometimes he says my name, but that name never reaches the world beyond his car. In school I take a nickname, while he calls me by my birth name. In school the kids call me *Kate* and the letters do not remind me of him.

I am safe. And thin. In beauty school we fix dinner at the end of every lesson — vegetables wilting like sylphs dying onstage. We eat carefully, admiring each other's manners, sticking to the assigned topics: movies, weather, domesticated animals, art.

And Him.

"The key to a successful date is to make him feel like a Great Man."

We learn to listen to men, to nod, to agree. We learn *yes yes yes* and *thank you please.*

Years later I take a self-defense class. The first thing the instructor asks us to do is scream. Around me women open their mouths and form the nameless syllables that signify fear. I open my mouth, too, widening the lips my grandmother bequeathed me, the bow-shaped lips that are the only thing linking me to her ghost, to the woman I believe would have understood me. I open my mouth and inhale, silent.

The instructor is gentle with me. But I leave the class crying because I cannot scream.

The man with the red car makes small talk with me, shies away from anything serious. Once I mention the word *abortion* and he frowns, so I know exactly how he feels. I am in tune with him, with his red car; I am empathetic and sympathetic both; I make him feel like a Great Man. In turn, he tells me I am beautiful, desirable, a rare flower.

But in the mirror at school, I do not look beautiful. His stubbled cheeks leave scratches, as if someone has struck a match against my skin. I am thin, thinner, thinnest. My friends and I pretend not to notice as each of us picks at her lunch.

One day I am in the bathroom, redoing my lips — two colors only, I do not have time for my mouth to vanish and return — when Jessica bustles in. I pretend I'm not watching as she rummages for change.

When her search fails, when her palms come up empty from her pockets, she turns to me and asks for what she needs in a surprisingly soft, low voice.

I am startled. No one — not one of my friends — still bleeds. No one weighs enough. It is understood that to bleed is to be fat.

I put the cap on my lipstick. She is looking at me and when I turn away from her eyes in the mirror, I look at the floor. It will be years before I understand that the something else she sees in my eyes before I turn away, the gaze that takes in her solid body, her incautious gestures, her gentle muscularity, is desire.

Yes yes yes.

Thank you.

I do.

Sometimes he asks why I'm so quiet. Once, we watch a film in which the heroine whispers sexy things to her husband. After the film is over, he picks at his hamburger. Then he says: "Can't you be more like that?"

I try.

I try to speak, to say things that will light the dark hum of the red car. But years later, in college, four boys will surround me on a dark walkway, surround me and begin, inexplicably, to tickle, then kiss me. The kisses will feel sharp, like needle pricks. And I will stand, shouting distance from a clump of passersby, shouting distance from students clustered at the steps of the library, and my throat will dry and my body will harden and I will not be able to make the sounds that might save me.

In high school I stop speaking. My teachers appreciate my polite, discreet presence. My teachers are men, and we do not read books by women. The women in the books we do read are quiet — victims, mothers, maids. My teachers tell me I am a good listener. They suggest I apply to Ivy League colleges like other promising students, white, wealthy students, students who have attended prep schools like mine, students like me.

Somehow I doubt the existence of others like me.

But I hide my sense of my difference. When my teachers comment admiringly on my poise, my sweetness, my dresses, I smile, knowing perfectly well by now what effect that has. I am a dancer. I know how to work an audience. At night, in the red car, I perform.

My real self, the girl between two names, is somewhere else.

Years later I will find that place useful for hiding, for avoiding the reality of a lover who has changed, her face mirroring the man who has stolen from her what I am also missing. The something else in her eyes will shift and smoke, becoming fear. I will watch her as she hovers over me, a dark triangle, watch my lover become the thing I am most afraid of, simply because she is afraid of me.

I will fantasize about killing him, her father. I will fantasize about it in great detail, until one day in my fantasy his face, the face I know only from photographs, becomes the face of the man with the red car.

At home, in the vestibular space of my bedroom, between my parents' world, the red car, dancing, and school, I write poems. In the poems I am water, and the man with the red car is a duck. I slide down his back in drops.

In my journal I write that I love him, that I want to marry him.

And so I stop eating, because I cannot find a way to reconcile the worlds I inhabit, and because starvation is the only speech I can afford.

Sometimes, like the goose girl in my favorite fairy tale, I speak to a familiar, hoping my familiar will answer. One day I am talking to the man with the red car. He is eating a sundae and I am watching. I ask him one of the questions they've taught us in beauty school: *if you were an animal, what would you be?*

He does not have to think it over. "A squirrel," he says, and I can tell he's proud. He slurps the last of his sundae through a straw. He does not ask what I would be.

I think, *I would be a man.*

It is 1986. When I move to New York City for college, I find the streets smeared with blood. There are bloody handprints everywhere, prints of names, names of politicians. I read the posters as I rush to the studio each morning — *Mayor Koch, Our Blood Is On Your Hands,* then a logo I don't understand, a pale pink triangle. *Act Up* it says, and *Silence = Death.* But death feels far away; silence, necessary.

In college I study English with a Great Man. I love his excitement at a strong line, a keen metaphor. I love his excitement, but when I whisper this to the girl next to me, he slams his hand on the podium.

"I won't have you talking about me," he says, his voice husky with cigarettes. Later, I learn that he is sleeping with her. He praises her body to us on the many days that she is absent.

After class, girls whisper to each other: *Don't let him shut the door to his office when he asks you in.* When the Great Man asks me in, I stand in the crevice the door makes, triangular, afraid of the bright light of his desk lamp and the blue light of his eyes. He hands me a copy of his latest book, then summons me closer so he can sign it. The book is complicated and clever; inside the word *lips* appears many times.

I take four classes with him so that I can learn to be a writer. We do not read a single woman author. Once someone asks why, waving his arm from the back row like an alarm that has suddenly decided to go off.

BLOOD : RED

The Great Man answers without losing his place in *The Waste Land*. "There are no British or American women writers worth reading."

"Dickinson?"

"Too domestic."

"Plath?"

"Too angry."

"Woolf?"

"Derivative."

"Stein?"

He laughs. "I think Stein's problem is self-evident."

I am sitting two rows from the front, vibrating with a new understanding of how a poem is composed. The Great Man has given me Stevens; he has given me Pound. He has also taught me the difference between bad and good poetry. When he asks us to write for his class, I know that I must not write about the man with the red car. That would be an angry poem, or maybe a domestic poem, or, worse, an angry domestic poem. That would be, I now know, a bad poem.

Instead I write sonnets about clouds, six each semester. Twenty-four poems about terrible weather. Sometimes, while I am writing, my pen skids to a stop before *nimbus,* before *cumulus.* Sometimes I see no point in finishing that week's poem, however fluffy the cloud, however silver its lining, simply because I am a woman, and women, as I now know, write bad poetry.

I get an A.

One of the boys asks me what I did to make the grade.

At night, after class, I ride the subway to my apartment. One of the girls from class rides as far as my stop. Often we sit across from each other, acknowledging each other's presence only by proximity. I know she sees me; I know she knows that I see her.

It takes me a month to realize who she reminds me of. By then I feel it, the something else I cannot name. There are jokes — gay people call it gaydar — about the thrill and terror of recognition, about its power. But there is no proper name for what I feel and, without a name, without witness, Jessica's bond with me vanishes, becomes wholly body, body and then energy, energy and then vibration, motion without signifier, unrecordable.

I do not see her.

The joke goes, "She could've saved you five years."

But I deny her. I turn from Jessica's new incarnation, this woman who sees through me, who inspires in me a charged knowledge that elaborates, magically, on something I do not yet claim. She sits across from me on the subway, dyke Christ to my Judas, vowing to haunt me. And I see Jessica after Jessica, year after year, until I finally give in and open my mouth in an ecstatic communion.

I come to hate studying. Thin, too thin, I have trouble concentrating. Words waver in front of my eyes. When I faint, the stairs to my brownstone redden and dissolve to dark.

For several days I cannot leave my apartment. Every time I begin a task, fears stall me, until unlocking the door is impossible. I pace, taking pieces of myself apart, until I am saved by a crack whore.

Her name is Corinne.

Her name is Corinne, and she lives down the hall. I know she is a whore because her clients ride the elevator with her, and because her pimp stalks her. Once, I step off the elevator to find him pounding on her door, first with a folding chair, then with his thick body.

"Corinne, goddammit, open the fucking door! Prazzie wants to see you, you shitty slut. Corinne!"

I know she does crack because she buys in the park two blocks away, out in the open the way crack deals happen in my neighborhood, her palm glowing with light, with the tiny glass vials.

The week I cannot leave my apartment, Corinne breaks the spell, pounding on my door one sweaty midnight. Her desperation does something to my nervous obsessiveness and I open the door in a rush of glad freedom. All she wants is rubbing alcohol. In exchange, she lets me visit her apartment to see her Murphy bed and seven cats.

I tell the man with the red car that there will be no more visits. His phone calls stalk me, plaintive and poignant, his grief at our breakup similar to the sound of the girls I dance with when they puke in the sink. Eventually the calls stop and the lies begin — lies to my parents, who still hope for a wedding.

I am distracted for the next several years. The man with the red car has distracted me. But I do not blame him. I look at my lips in the mirror — bow-shaped, like my grandmother's. She was a singer, but instead of a voice, she bequeathed me her lips.

Her name was Buena Vista — *good view.*

Her marriage to my grandfather saved the family farm.

I like my lips. I do not blame him, the man with the red car, for wanting to touch them. I look in the mirror every morning before I make up my face with all that red. Sometimes, thinking of Tara, I touch myself.

The smile I see isn't mine.

It will be years before I bleed again, before the color red means something else. It will be years before I drive myself, long hours on a deserted highway, to see a woman with red hair. It will be years before someone watches me eat, watches my lips with a stare that is neither calculated nor appraising, but wicked. It will be years before wickedness appeals to me, before I stop wearing pink, before a red car means little or nothing, before the face in the mirror opens its plain mouth to speak.

"Do you have anything darker?" my girlfriend asks the skeptical blonde behind the counter. We are shopping for lipstick because I want to kiss her and leave prints.

"I'll go check," the salesgirl says, and heads for the back of the store. She does not return.

So we steal things — silver eyeliner, blue nail polish, men's cologne. For a week, on a dare, my lover and I wear blue nail polish until it scabs off and we find ourselves picking at it with our teeth. But for that week, her hands on my flesh look like bruises, as if someone has hit my thighs, arms, belly. Her hands on my flesh look ugly, and I beg her to remove the color, to make her nails clear again.

For our beauty school graduation dinner, we're instructed to bring something fattening — something *sinful*, Glory Sue says. I bake a pumpkin pie. When it is cool, I cover it in plastic, tucking in its edges.

Years later, I will enter my lover's kitchen, lured by a sweet, cinnamon scent, buttery and warm. "Pie," she says. "Sweet potato." We stand in the kitchen, sipping coffee, waiting for it to cool. When it is done, she cuts two large slices and motions me to join her. She walks through the kitchen, living room, hallway. I follow her, and I follow the pie. She pushes open the door to our bedroom with her shoulder, flicks the light with her wrist. Then she sets both plates on the bedstand and sits on the quilt.

The slices are wrapped; for a moment I think she wants me to touch and taste through plastic. Instead she smiles, removing the barrier.

The beauty school classroom mirrors are veiled in gauzy streamers; at the center of the room is a table draped in silver cloth. We place our pies, cakes, cookies, and pastries in a seductive chorus line and then stand, soldiers at a peep show.

We wait for the word.

Eat.

We expect to hear it any minute. But we are well-trained; we do not flinch. We watch each other through the streamer-draped mirror and do not know that we are watching hunger.

Glory Sue hands each of us a rolled-up certificate, stamped with a red seal. Her lips part. Again we expect it: *Eat.* Instead she stands with her back against the table. "Girls," she says, and she does not mean *women,* "thank you for your participation."

Years later a student enters my office and drops a paper on my desk. Before I glance at it, she rolls up her sleeves. Outside, it is raining; the light in my office is pewter-blue. Through the gloom, I notice that her arms are covered with bracelets. As my vision adjusts, I realize they are scars.

Her name is sweet; her hands are graceful. In the faint light we look at each other and do not say a word. We do not need to; we speak the way women have always spoken to each other. My face tells her I will remember; her body tells me she trusts nobody.

When she leaves, her inked-up paper clutched so tight I know her scars must sting, I bend my head to my book again. I try to bring myself back, back to language, back to the words that will make her tale untrue. I try to read my way out of what I've seen, but the letters won't

40 *BLOOD : RED*

let me. Late late nights and early mornings I write, trying desperately to communicate without using my body, sick of knowing only one language, the language of flesh and blood and pain. I want access to the words men use. I want in, into the club, where the light is strong and arms can carry someone. I want to enter. And I realize that I have known this from the beginning.

Glory Sue's lips part again.

"Touch yourselves."

We look down, at our red shoes.

"Touch yourselves." She puts her hands on her waist. "I want you to feel how fat food has made you. *This*," and she pinches her flesh until her fingers are full, "is cake. *This* is pie. Feel it. Feel your fatness. Feel how much of yourself you would like to slice off."

At first we're shy. We aren't used to our own skin. Mine feels flaky, dry, crusted. Beside me, Tara gnaws on her thumb. But soon someone puts a hand on her upper arm.

"I hate this," she says. "How it jiggles. I wish I could cut it off."

Jasmine puts one hand on her hips; someone else cups her breasts in both hands and bends forward. I touch my nose. Tara puts both hands on her legs; I see her in the mirror. I watch as she runs both hands up and down her thighs, over and over. Soon I follow, imitating her, running my hands up and down my thighs, over and over, along with her, dispossessing my flesh. We touch ourselves, cutting our limbs in half, winnowing and winnowing, and it feels, even now, describing it, like bloody handprints marking every inch wretched.

I see Tara in the mirror, undoing herself. She is watching her own hands, her own eyes. But in the midst of our feast, her gaze meets mine. We stare at each other in the glass, we stare, and the cutting, the severing, the slicing and winnowing become something else. I watch her watch me, my hands on my thighs, and I watch her hands reply, parting her lips.

It will be years before I can name the something else in her eyes, before a woman names the something else in mine. It will be years before I can name it: *desire*; years before a woman bleeds into my hands and I think *yes yes* this is what blood is for, salt and not cotton, *yes yes* this and not children, *yes yes* and *please.* It will be years before I learn to scream, before my name matches the mirror, before the words I speak spell something besides *rape* and the foods I eat become poetry; it will be years before I name the difference, name it *desire,* name it *anger,* name it after a color women feel but cannot see.

Yellow

I am holding a cat too tightly in my lap. With one hand I am brushing its tabby-rainbow, admiring its sheen. What I remember: the rust-tint of age spots, soft hands on my hands.

My mother, my sister and I have travelled from North Carolina to a battered corner of Illinois to visit my mother's mother in her cozy, quirky stone house. At ten I don't know the history of Grandma Graflund's tragedy — the car wreck that killed her husband and stole from her something intangible, visible only as sheen on a CAT scan. She is forgetting, stroke by stroke, snapshots from a life: Hi-Mac candy, Tante Haase, kick-the-can.

At ten I don't know what it means to forget your daughter's name and then your own.

Ella. Ella Pauline. I have a photograph — Ella with two girlfriends, ankle-length skirts bobbing above white socks, tennis rackets slung over sturdy shoulders. In another, her father stands in a field, overalls stained with chicken feed, chickens nipping swollen denim, his toothless mouth frozen open, as if the camera were a gun.

It is the last day my mother will ever speak with her mother and be understood. All the long drive North the radio blares Tony Orlando and Dawn's "Tie a Yellow Ribbon," telling the story of a man returning to his beloved, asking her to tie a yellow ribbon around a tree if she's still in love. Grandma's oak is wound with yellow string.

After orange punch and chocolate cookies I sit her tabby in my lap, determined to brush it smooth. But I brush it backwards, because I don't understand the chronology of fur.

Grandma places her hand over mine and gets me brushing in the right direction. "Cats don't like to be brushed backwards, Callie. They're always moving forward. Keep going. That's right. Keep moving on."

I let my hand go beneath her hand, lulled by the motion, till the cat's fur glints smooth. Still we keep brushing. The cat purrs and Grandma's hand is warm as summer and I know in that moment what I want, what will lure me. Hand-over-hand, till what's backwards is present tense, till what's ruffled is soft again, till I'm part of another person.

By the time we pull out of the driveway, I understand the difference between good-bye and *good-bye*.

Black

I was born a ghost, guardian of a dead woman's lips, so I've always been resistant to chronology. Time works best when you think of it as gravity: tugging weighty objects to the bottom of the river.

I lie for a living. Every storyteller is a liar, even if the tales they set out to tell are true. *Buena Vista.* Good view. She married a Canadian, his surname *Guess,* the shape of flax-colored geese flying a question mark over terrible rivers.

There are ghosts who return, like a betrayed lover, and ghosts who encrypt themselves, like my father's mother, Buena Vista Brabham. She bequeathed me her mouth: bow-shaped lips that shard sparks. I lie for a living because my lips aren't my own.

Loveliness at the World's Fair. Sipping Coke with a millionaire, her dark hair piled high.

A flock of birds against a pewter sky.

I have a photograph. Vista's long dead, but in the snapshot she's smiling. So is her husband, my grandfather Harry Guess. They're in love, honeymooning. She isn't pregnant yet; she doesn't know she's diabetic. She doesn't know she'll die in pain, though when the doctor calls Harry into his office, he will lie about the blood, about her cries.

In the photograph, Vista and Harry wear safe, white smiles. And so I love the shot, because it's proof that someone in my past lived in the present, tasting sugar.

Even if it killed her.

How can I not love the dead?

I hear the door open, the doctor's footsteps down the white-tiled hall. Harry sits, smiling, anticipating a son or daughter. Harry, now Senior. He refused to wear black. Instead he learned lullabies and sewed his son's booties. We have letters: *Harry Junior eats his bits of bacon with a fork. Harry Junior can say "horse" and "negress."* Harry Senior wore white suits. His accent was Canadian; his last name, a question. There were wheat fields when the oil wells dried, but by then it didn't matter. By then Harry Senior was dead of cancer and my father had learned how to say "ghost."

Vista's sister Dorothy was married to Harry Senior on his deathbed for a sum of money and an elaborate house in Forest Hills, New York. In exchange she promised to raise her sister's infant as her son. The first thing she did was dress baby Harry in black, to mourn the husband she'd never touched and the sister she'd lost. The second thing she did was to invest the money wisely. The third thing she did was to sell the house and move back to Bamberg, South Carolina.

Dorothy raised my father from her slump on the sofa, where she watched the walls and then TV. Her maid Rene taught my father conversation. And warmth. And human connectedness.

can say "negress"

Rene's son was a construction worker. On days when sighs freeze, construction workers gather around trash barrels smoldering with cautious paper fires, warming their hands over the steam. Some years back, Rene's son, whose name I do not know, stood with his hands stretched over red sparks. When I think of him, I think of myth — Moses and the burning bush, Christ's stigmata, fire flickering a liar's kiss. The flames caught, nibbling his gloves, sweater, throat. He cried fire, became fire, became the element the ambulance came for. Soon Rene's son was en route, a true light stoking the glare of traffic.

He suffered second-degree burns — nothing he ought to have died from. But the ambulance driver was white, and took his time. The dark man stretched the length of the van was not a priority. And so the driver circuited a maze around the city. By the time he got to the hospital he thought best suited — a dark hospital in a dark neighborhood — Rene's son's burns had set fire to his blood. Second-degree turned third turned fatal. Her son was dead, but the white hospital was clean.

Buena Vista. My father is interested in burns, which killed Rene's son, and diabetes, which killed his mother, and prostate cancer, which killed his father. He's interested in ghosts; we have this in common. In another snapshot, Vista's lips purse to a question. Her hair is bobbed; she might be a flapper. But her shawl is pure Victoriana; even in dress, she was torn between two eras.

Buena Vista died in childbirth. My father grew up believing that he was responsible for his mother's death, that if he was naughty, the women tending to him would crumple, bloody. My father learned to be good to save the thousand mothers of his desperate dreams.

Today my father is a stoic man, fair in everything, most ethical, most gentle. Gentleness is worn into him in grooves — he learned it the hard way. He doesn't lie. But lies were worn into him in grooves, and I learned lying from the easy way our family avoids honest history, from the strange faces everyone wears when we visit Dorothy: his stepmother, my Nana, now in a nursing home, but still able, with one word, to transform my father into *orphan*.

Nana took her dead husband's name and her dead sister's title, becoming *Mrs. Harry A. Guess, Sr.* Vista's story was lost, smoothed over. When I learned why relatives at family reunions approach me with outstretched arms, sleepwalkers circuiting a maze of history; when I learned why I am gazed at like a ghost, my life began to make sense.

I look exactly like Vista, save for my hair, which is as light as hers was dark. I grew up knowing I was haunted, treated as if I was haunted. And that is the South, for me — every white woman's face the face of memory.

Spanish moss is silver at dusk, black at midnight, blue-grey at sunrise. No matter what its color, it is delicate and shadowy, suggesting to me the long drives of my childhood summers, drives through impossibly dense, swampy forest.

My sister and I call the moss "ghost lace," and think it far more beautiful than the lace on our velvet dresses. But when our father tugs strands from a tree, we are disappointed by its stiffness, its brittle fragility. Like Nana's shellacked beehive hairdo it looks silky, but feels coarse and dry to the touch.

I am nine, my sister is six, and we have just survived a long summer drive to Bamberg by playing Martian for seven hours. We invented the game ourselves. First we shift around in the backseat until we are upside-down, our blonde ponytails scraping the floor of the car. Then we hook our feet over the seatback. From this vantage point, with the sometimes painful heat of the floor searing our backs, the upside-down world becomes the view

BLOOD : BLACK

from a spaceship. We are astronauts, scanning the sky for wayward Martians.

When we start this game, our parents cringe. We can hear them cringe; it's audible. Everything we see through the window becomes a spacecraft of some kind or, better, a Martian. Only truly weird things can be Martians; Martians are a find. When we pass Bubba's Bar-B-Q or the Piggly-Wiggly, we roar in unison, "Get back, you dummy Martian pighead!" As the floating swine vanish in our sturdy craft's wake, we congratulate each other on a job well done.

When we arrive at Nana's, our parents barter with her for an hour's rest. My sister and I are shepherded out of our tiny car and into Nana's blue Cadillac. Nana waits in the driveway, fanning herself with her rhinestone sunglasses until the AC kicks in and the car is cool. Then we toodle — there is no other word for her slow, inaccurate driving — the five blocks to Ziggy's restaurant. She hustles us inside quickly, reminding us of the dangers of too much light.

Soon we are eating fried chicken and mashed potatoes. Cups of lime jello with perforated carrots appear as if by magic. My sister sits beside me, pouring salt into her grits and picking fatback out of limp green beans. Periodically Nana tugs on my collar, bidding me to face her as she repins my barrettes. My sister and I have our mother's thin, limp hair. It is flyaway white in winter, chlorine green in summer. Barrettes slide through the strands and land in our collars. This summer I have lost two blue butterflies, four pink swans, one yellow cat. My grandmother clasps the plastic clips in clumps of hair behind my ears; when they fall down the back of my dress they feel cool, like her hands, or the ice in the Cokes she drinks all day.

I am on my second skin. I don't like the taste of meat, but I like the crispy, paprika-scented chicken skin, all grease and batter, and peel it away from the white meat beneath. Once I have collected a pile on the side of my plate, I drop each piece into my palm daintily. Then I cram the lot into my mouth.

This is my status when another little girl walks into Ziggy's, holding her mother's hand and scuffing bare feet against battered linoleum.

Nowadays when I stare I don't necessarily open my mouth and drool, but at nine that is the gesture that accompanies gawking. I open my mouth and bits of chicken skin fall out. I am covered with grease, a greasy girl, a flyaway, greasy white girl, my hair limp at my nape, my eyes the blandest blue possible.

The girl bends into her mother's waist.

The man behind the counter looks disgruntled as he hands over their takeout order. I am not the only customer staring, stopped. The girl's mother counts out change without letting go of her daughter's hand, then exits quickly into the exhausting heat of a South Carolina July.

As the door squeals shut, the restaurant resumes its gossip-chatter. I undo the damages, picking bits of

BLOOD : BLACK

chicken skin out of my lap, grabbing the salt cellar from my sister and hitting her on the shoulder.

"Stupid farthead," I say. "You made me spit out my food."

As my sister begins to cry, my grandmother intercedes, sliding her pie in front of Alison smoothly, handing her a clean fork. Alison stops crying and stuffs filling into her mouth until the pie is gone. A pile of pecans — she will only swallow Karo syrup and flaky crust — rises on chipped white china.

Later I will hit her again and call her a dumb blonde. But for now I am busy pushing my plate away, wiping my hands on paper napkins, sucking ketchup off my thumbs. In school I've learned how to braid thick cotton strips for the rug our whole class is making together. I love the motion of braiding, how my hands crisscross and then return. The wave of it. My wrists can do it; it feels natural. Though my hair is a hundred times thinner than the cotton strips, I separate out three flimsy strands and cross them, seeking beauty, seeking the new life beauty will give me, wanting to bend into my mother's waist like the beautiful girl whose face is burned into my memory.

My grandmother catches my wrists and squeezes.

It is not the sting of her rings at my wrists, but the sting of her words: "Good girls don't braid their hair," she says, and then something else, advice that will haunt me. "Only nigger girls braid their hair. If you braid your hair, people will think you're a nigger."

I remember her laughter but not her tone. She thought it was funny; speaking of "Negroes" was always cause for humor with my grandmother. Now, envisioning myself at nine — a skinny, anemic kid with skin the color of chicken meat and hair the color of absence — I sometimes find myself laughing, too. The possibility that braiding my wispy hair might somehow transform me — alter family ties, purify my white Southern history — seems weirdly optimistic, as if my grandmother could foresee that someday I would feel this angry at the ugly history of my father's family.

I let my hands fall into my lap. After lunch, when two miniature boxes of chocolate creams emerge from the mysterious depths of Nana's purse, I tear into the candy as if to make up for the braiding motions she's denied me. I tear into it, as my sister tears into hers, poking out the bottoms of chocolates, squishing them to watch the fillings ooze, rolling them around on my tongue, feeling their shapes before biting down.

When the cashier whistles at us on the way out I smile coyly and twirl my hair. But the girl's face remains burned into my memory. She will haunt me, as I will not haunt her. My memory of her is the negative — that which changes, develops, and yet preserves the past — from which my family's whiteness emerges.

Stark, stinking of chemicals, inflexible.

BLOOD : BLACK

My father grew up in Bamberg, raised by his aunt Dorothy, the woman I call my grandmother, my Nana. His family history is tragically convoluted and gothic. The usual Faulknerian ingredients abound — betrayal, historical inaccuracy, miscegenation, incest, financial scams, and especially insanity. Since we rarely visited my mother's family — the cousins I now count myself close to — my father's family came to feel like The Family. For better or worse I thought of myself, and sometimes still think of myself, as a Southerner.

Certainly they were interesting, my Southern relations. One of my cousins sold high-powered speedboats to drug runners *and* the federal agents pursuing them; he once took me and my sister for a body-boggling boat ride in a tiny craft powered by an airplane engine. Another cousin was a brilliant cartoonist and animated filmmaker, once nominated for an Oscar. Like many of my father's relations, he went mad at a very young age and then lived for a long, long time, trekking from relative to relative, drinking vast quantities of tea and concocting conspiracy theories based on the relation between the height of the pyramids and the width of the moon.

The women on my father's side seemed more stable than the men, something that might have been reassuring if they'd been at all nice. But some of them were bitter social climbers, angry still that the South had lost The War Between The States.

The oddest thing about these Southern women was their mix of strength and weakness, a mix I suppose in some ways I've inherited. If any of them had been lesbians, I'd have called them Power Femmes for the ferocity of their passivity. Take Aunt Julia, for example. Aunt Julia (who is always referred to only as Aunt Julia, so I have no idea what her last name was or how we are related) was a fine Southern lady living in Barnwell, South Carolina during the 1860's. Aunt Julia's story is meant to demonstrate her strength, represented (because it is more feminine) as stubbornness. Told to evacuate her home because Sherman's troops and fires were fast approaching, she stamped her foot and said, "I won't leave without my piano." Of course, she got her way. Someone trundled up the piano and took it on the road. Satisfied, Aunt Julia agreed to leave the front parlor for a spell.

Years after I first heard this story, my father and I were walking the dog along a quiet South Carolina beach. As Puff loped gleefully off in search of dead fish, my father literally smote his forehead with his palm.

"Cal, I never thought of this before. My family is a matriarchy."

"Duh," I said.

It has always seemed odd to me that my lesbianism shocks my father's, and not my mother's, family. So many of my female Southern relations seemed not only in control of the men in their lives, but uninterested in them. From this reality came my first lessons about sex, passed along like salt-and-pepper shakers. After visiting married cousins with separate bedrooms: "When you get married, don't sleep away from your husband like that. If he doesn't get it at home, he'll go elsewhere."

There was a kind of sheen to frigidity among my Southern family. Women were supposed to hate sex; it was considered perfectly acceptable to broadcast this. Oddly, the vulgarity of these proclamations fit in smoothly with the beauty and delicacy of several of my Southern relatives' lives — with bone-thin china, mahogany furniture, well-coiffed gardens. The lives they led seemed then, and seem now, to be miraculously luxurious, obscenely and indecently so. Sometimes the lushness, the fat, was so rich it was hard to breathe. The taboo on anything sexual seemed to allow, or even generate, an emphasis on physical luxury so intense that time spent among these people had the feel of living underwater.

In Bamberg, this was less true only because my grandmother, a single woman and a terrible miser, lived in a relatively modest two-bedroom house into which she could cram only so much luxury. Too, the likelihood of becoming spoiled in a dirt-poor, heartlost, dusty town like Bamberg was slim. Nana's attempts at aristocracy, fervent as they were, came across as eccentricity, even cruelty.

Things were different with my cousins in Savannah, Georgia, whom we visited at Thanksgiving, Christmas, and once or twice each summer. In their elegant brownstone, often featured on postcards as "the heart of old Savannah," luxury was naturalized; beauty was organic to the ivy-covered brick and gilt wallpaper. Everything was embroidered with initials, as if there was a possibility something might get lost. At Thanksgiving we feasted on salmon instead of turkey; each place setting boasted a silver salt boat, symmetrically aligned with a tiny silver spoon.

I became a writer on those trips to visit my Southern relatives. Some of my training involved long storytelling sessions, jousts really, often in unintelligible Southern accents, with hors d'oeuvres for props. Almost everyone on my father's side of the family is an incredible oral wordsmith. But it wasn't only the narratives and crazy characters I absorbed that let me fall in love with words. What shaped my development as a writer during those endless vacations was the sense, which I've felt for as long as I can remember, that I was an outsider.

I suspect most artists feel this; in order to create art, you have to collect material by observing the world around you. Everything that happens, happens twice: once to the person, human; once to the artist, inhumane. Perhaps I would have been less inclined to write if I had fit smoothly into the weave of my father's family. But I recognized early on that I needed to make use of my outsiderness, or my heart would snap like benne wafers. I began searching for ways to articulate the gap I saw between my relations' verbal depictions of themselves and their actual behavior.

The most significant examples of deconstructing familial myths happened in Nana's house. Every year we'd pull into the driveway, my sister and I rumpled from Martian-games, and tumble into Nana's arms. Every year my sister and I whispered behind cupped hands that we did not want to be kissed by Nana — no, not kissed at all. She'd cup our cheeks in the vise of her hands, smooshing them together till our lips puckered. The kiss, when it came, had all the force of the lost war behind it. And she was obsessed with the war, which my small sister for a time believed the South had won — obsessed with the way of life she felt had been stolen from her.

I remember her living room, furniture arranged in a neat L around a giant television. I remember watching Nana's maid, Rene, dust the slick glass of a picture frame, its edges gilt. Beneath the glass was pseudo-parchment: a replica of the Declaration of Succession my ancestors had signed.

Years later, as a teaching assistant in a women's studies class, I watched seventy college students struggle with Toni Morrison's *The Bluest Eye*. New to teaching, desperate to please a professor I adored, I tried hard to contain my own fierce emotional response to the book. And so I made the mistake I've since tried to unlearn — approaching lessons from a distance, as if nothing we read or said moved me personally. I treated the book aesthetically, praising Morrison's elegant and precise prose, dissecting its structure. But I didn't admit that the book had broken something inside of me, that I cried over it, that I saw myself and my father in its portrayal of privileged white children tended to by black women at the terrible expense of their own children.

Nana saw no irony in asking her maid to dust the document that signified our family's ties to the violent oppression of Rene's family. In fact, Nana saw no irony in anything, and yet even as tiny girls my sister and I recognized something awry in the way she treated Rene. We were no saints; we stole from Rene all the love our parents and Nana withheld or mislaid. But we noticed Rene's cowed demeanor, her dropped glances, her air of solitude. I never learned the color of her eyes or their wisdom because she never looked me straight on.

My sister and I were sweet, rosy-cheeked little white girls. In Bamberg and Savannah, sweet, rosy-cheeked little white girls from upper-middle class families grow up to be debutantes. Debutantes marry lawyers and senators' sons. Debutantes reenact tacit segregation, sending their rosy-cheeked children to posh, private, all-white schools, moving into the better neighborhoods, hiring black folks to feed, clean, clothe, and pamper them.

I grew up loving Rene more than my grandmother, who was not really my grandmother, though I did not learn that until much later: one of so many secrets and lies I would come to mimic. I learned storytelling at my Southern family's feet, but I also learned to lie. Years later, when I lied to a lover, when I betrayed her in another woman's arms, I would have to retrace that gesture — the ease of it, the luxury of flicking truth away like dust. White lies seemed insignificant even as they accumulated. And I would track and track until I realized that it was truth, not lying, that was rare in my childhood.

In the midst of writing this I am watching lovers' lies played out on a grand scale as the president of the United States is impeached for having lied about an extramarital affair. I have watched his face, shadows shifting across it; watched him lie, watched him lie about lying. I feel a terrible kinship with this man, a kinship I do not want to feel. I can't pretend, any longer, that I do not know what it means to lie, or to lie to cover up a first lie.

I am trying to learn how to be honest. Until recently, I thought I was. And I am learning that this is the worst lie of all — to think oneself honest as one lies about exactly that.

As a lesbian, I have found few models for honesty. My government lies to queers and forces them to lie in return. The lies I am speaking of are entrenched — lies like the Defense of Marriage Act, sodomy laws, and the "Don't Ask, Don't Tell" policy of the US military. The fundamental structure of gay life in contemporary American culture is a lie, as Eve Sedgwick has pointed out. The love that dare not speak its name both does and doesn't, and does both loudly.

Those lies are inhaled with the very air. But I also learned to lie as an artist — to lie for a living, to write fiction. And while as a feminist and a lesbian I see through the lies above, as an artist I often find it difficult to sort through accuracy and embellishment. I owe my artist-self the freedom to spin wild tall tales, to invent lives and events, to stretch true situations into wicked, funny stories. If I try to be precise and perfect, my gift dries up; words no longer love me.

Part of the process of creation is altering reality. Some artists — realist painters, for instance — attempt to capture reality as if in a mirror. But this is not the sort of art that interests me. Years ago, as a ballet dancer, I fell in love with George Balanchine's choreography precisely because he did away with the banal pseudo-realism of story ballets — with plot, character, realist detail. The truth in his ballets came from abstraction, from sound and repetition, from variations on a theme. I value abstraction more than realism because I value passion, and passion's exaggerations, and passion's speed.

How then to be true to my artist-self, to Carol, when I am also Cassie — the family Cassandra, the truth-teller who pays the price for speaking out against injustice?

As an artist, I feel in myself the tendency to lie at every turn. I so want my stories to live — to be lively — that the desire to embellish them is impossible to ignore. For example, we do have letters describing my grandfather's care for my father. But while Harry Jr. learned to eat bacon, he did not learn to say *negress.*

Actually, my father didn't speak until he was three; for a time, people thought he was retarded. Then one day he ambled into the living room and announced calmly — his first words — *I am a master carpenter.*

That's true.

Except maybe he wasn't three, but four. Except maybe it wasn't the living room, but the kitchen.

Which lies matter? Which truths are necessary? And which lies are, themselves, beautiful — the lie Matisse told when he sketched a woman's body like a scarf and painted her blue; the lie Stein told when she titled one of her books *The Autobiography of Alice B. Toklas?*

Lying, I am learning, is not the same as using your imagination.

My family has lied to black folks for generations.

I loved Rene, but loving Rene was letting myself be lied to. My sister and I spent hours in Rene's arms, or sitting at her feet while she cooked fried chicken. We spent hours listening to her soft voice, smelling her floury skirts, learning the gospel, memorizing mottos: *God's will for us is ever sweet.* For our birthdays each year, she sent us flowery Hallmark cards with smiling white children on the cover, their blue eyes sparkling. Inside, she'd tuck two fives or a ten.

I learned later that the money actually came from my parents. Every year at Christmas, they gave Rene money on the sly. Rene promptly purchased greeting cards, tucked the bills inside, and mailed them off in time for our January birthdays.

Nana gave us silverware. Every year, a knife.

My sister and I made our way through the world, attending costly private high schools, donning prom gowns, teasing our wispy hair, traipsing off to prestigious colleges and then borrowing from our parents as we pursued elaborate artistic schemes (me, the writer; my sister, the musician).

The last time I saw my father's family was several years ago at Christmas. One of my Savannah cousins was newly engaged, and so of course much of the holiday was spent teasing me and my sister about when our turns would come. I have been out to my family for years, but to keep things calm with my Savannah relations, I remained mute. I remember being introduced to several eligible bachelors, all of whom turned their faces from me quickly — me, the grubby one, the bohemian. I spent most of my time in the kitchen, talking with Zelie, my cousins' maid.

When I teach *Incidents in the Life of a Slave Girl*, I point out to students that it is the mistress, not the master, who bends over Harriet's bed. It is the mistress who whispers to Harriet as a man might, as if the mistress were a rapist, which, in that moment, she becomes.

I grew up watching Nana watching Rene.

I believe that Nana and I have some things in common.

In the garden of her old blue house, Spanish moss silvered like family secrets; the clump highest up was shaped like a noose. As daylight faded, it sloughed blues to glint and then pewter, but my sister and I learned not to tug it down. It felt chalky and left marks — first a terrible itch, then small blood-swells like pimples. Redbugs. There's a penalty for getting too close.

On my last visit to Bamberg I paced Nana's garden, thinking up stories, feeling honesty itchy and just out of reach. Then my parents descended into the taut grass and still-lush greenyness of a South Carolina winter garden, and untangled the ivy that had grown over the gate.

"You're so angry, Carol," my family says. But the essence of anger, to me, is my cousins taking a woman — Rene, about whose life I will never know a single true thing — and stuffing her into a maid's uniform, tight as a straitjacket, binding her hands with hot pads, forcing her to stare day in, day out, at bubbling pots till the steam blinds her. My anger is about this act of inventing lives for people and imposing those invented lives over their real ones, and then using what power you have to make those ugly invented lives come true. For the inventions my Southern relations practice are not the inventions of an artist. The lives they make up are not the same as the ones I make up on paper or in my head.

I inherited my storytelling gifts from my father's family. I inherited great passion, and a superb imagination. But I also inherited fear, the fear of someone who's watched those great gifts be twisted and perverted, used against others until those others buckled and broke.

The last time I talked to Nana was on the telephone. The conversation was predictable: first, we talked about the weather, not in the states we live in, but in Missouri and Mississippi. The weather channel is one of Nana's hobbies; she tracks disasters with a cat's keen eyes. Then she teased me about my boyfriend. I don't have a boyfriend, am openly gay, but no matter. Next, she tried to get me to join the Daughters of the American Revolution. The first time she asked, I actually tried to explain why I wasn't interested. I didn't get far, though, because my mother grabbed the phone and began talking about the weather in Mississippi, her voice sweet as syrup, eyes glazed.

My family humors Nana, my mother especially. And this is another thing I can't bear to witness. My mother bears the brunt of my father's family's snobbishness. Born to German and Swedish farming families, she was raised in poverty in a suburb of Chicago. She remembers wearing flour-sack dresses and not being able to go to the dentist despite terrible problems with her teeth. My mother's father worked for a candy factory, but lost his job when war rationing shut it down. My mother's family struggled, starved. Yet it has always been made clear — in the subtle way that my Southern relations make things clear — that they think my father married beneath his station. Never mind that he and my mother adore each other, have been married for over thirty years, and are perhaps the most stable marriage in the history of his family. I grew up knowing that my mother was slighted, in small and large ways, among my Southern relations.

What made this unbearable was watching her take it.

When Nana calls her a Nazi, my mother ignores it. She never fights back, but smiles harder, hugs Nana tighter. I grew up watching my mother deny anger she must've felt, watching her become sweeter and sweeter, till now I hardly recognize myself in her.

I am not sweet. I am angry most of the time. In this respect, I am much like my Southern relations. Their anger, however, is at the audacity of uppity blacks and white trash, at threats to the good life they led when folks knew their place. My anger is at their audacity, at the good life that continues to regenerate itself, at the status quo in the South that seems so ideologically entrenched that I feel a paralyzing sense of hopelessness when I visit.

It is harder and harder to go home.

When we visit my grandmother, I think of the silver lover whose gestures I've incorporated into my own. Not because Nana is girlish — given half a chance, she'd have made a stunning butch — but because Nana, like me, has incorporated history and more history, so that now her body is an album. She is fat, Nana, and fat is a four-letter word in my family's vocabulary. To be fat (for a woman; men have different rules) is to take up too much space, need too much, desire everything. But I see Nana's fatness as other than hunger. I think Nana and I are similar, much as I am sometimes loathe to admit it.

I think Nana, too, incorporates women. Starting with her sister. I think she misses her.

Nana tends to her body as widows tend to their lovers' ashes. In her fatness are her ghosts — for ghosts are not transparent, but take up space — and her shame at being haunted. Over and over loss buffeted her — the sister she envied, the husband she tolerated, the son she abused, the maidservant she might have desired. No one stayed. Not the Old South, not my father, not her granddaughters. She planted herself, as if roots could protect her, and in that stillness she grew stubbornness. I understand ardor, and fear of change. When I say that Nana is one of the most passionate people I've ever met, I mean it.

In trying to understand what good things have come to me from my Southern relations, in trying to acknowledge their kindnesses as well as their culpability and my own accountability for oppression and cruelty, I've come to believe that the good gift is passion. All that political fervor, determination, belief in "the cause," all that stubbornness I see in myself, albeit directed towards very different causes.

Passion turned in on itself becomes not necessarily repression, but incorporation. To incorporate is to be haunted. And they are all haunted; all of the South is haunted. This is the beauty and tragedy tourists do not see. The ghosts are there, but hesitant, slow to surface, surfacing only when they believe they are safe.

They are safe when they know they will be seen.

Nana is haunted. But it's not only her sister's face that she remembers. When she looks in the mirror, I suspect she sees Rene's eyes. I believe that she loved her. I believe that their relationship could've been other, could've been affection. And I believe that the thing stolen from Rene is irreplaceable.

I have come to hate my yellow hair. It will not braid; it will not curl. Instead it hangs, limp as unread pages in a banal book. My lover begs me to keep my hair long so she can run her fingers through it, tug on it, muss it, feel strands like gold silk. So she can handle it, contain it, admire its dead weight.

Hair is dead, like nails, like flakes of skin. The things we use to divide ourselves each from each — the things we use to measure beauty — are often dead. When I look in the mirror, I see pale skin, pallor, hair the color of dirty water. I don't see gold and I don't see silver.

I don't want to haunt anyone. If there's anything we are put on earth to do, it's to make life easier for others — to stop or lessen suffering. I don't think incorporation does that for anyone but the individual.

I believe in communication.

But before there can be communication, there must be revision. There must be a rewriting of myth and tradition. When I brush my hair, I feel its weight. I am not a dumb blonde, not a debutante. But there is no erasing color, no erasing the knowledge of what was stolen from so many generations of African-Americans.

As a writer, I seek to fill in the lines of the skeleton some white Southern men and women have misnamed "truth" with bold color, as if filling in my bow-shaped lips with crimson in a well-lit mirror.

Neon

Two men exit a long, white limo and hurry down our straggly front lawn, making a beeline for me and my sister. This is my memory of almost being kidnapped when I was eleven, my mother appearing just in time to run us inside. Our dog Puff was almost kidnapped too, by a cult that sacrificed white animals. She was saved only to be humped by a Scotty dog while my sister and I watched in fascination and disgust. My parents wisely decided against Spitz-Scotty puppy combos and we learned the word "abortion." Later Alison and I incorporated our dramatic kidnap-rescue saga into the clattery roller skate shows we choreographed to ABBA, the Bee Gees, Blondie, and the Doobie Brothers on the slick linoleum of our tiny front room.

Our two years in Miami remain vivid in my mind, both because there were more than the usual assortment of freaky bits, and because fifth grade is the last childhood year I recall with any accuracy. In sixth grade I caved in on myself. I remember snippets; snippets, which is more than I can say for seventh or eighth. They're gone, if they ever existed. Not eating for extended periods of time does something to either short- or long-term memory.

But Miami. My father moved the family again because a Ph.D. in mathematics from Stanford was not enough to satisfy his ambition. Ever the overachiever, he'd gone from working under Admiral Rickover designing nuclear submarines to pioneering long-distance telephone technology at Bell Labs. I used to brag about my father, saying he had numbers named after him. Actually, it's a formula; I have no idea what it does. I couldn't make my mind wrap around numbers at all. They had no emotions, nothing I could feel, toss, taste. Ultimately, my father came to agree. The beautiful numbers he juggled on bulky computers in the 1970's failed to satisfy his appetite and he returned to school to become a medical doctor — to integrate theory and practice, to exorcise his ghosts by counting cures.

So we moved again, this time to Miami, where my father joined an accelerated MD program. All of the participants had Ph.D.'s and some background in science. But the program was — even at eleven I discerned this — impossibly difficult, depressing, and sadistic. I remember my father's face thinning to shadows, parts of him vanishing. And the freak quotient among his classmates! The students I met didn't act like grown-ups, but they didn't act like kids, either. One couple was obsessed with hygiene and wore face masks 24-7. They were mocked by a stubby woman who trailed long blonde wigs and pirouetted around our kitchen, tickling or hitting on anyone who got in her way.

There was a great distinction between the men in the program (it was mostly men), and the wives, who at times resembled war widows (they had T-shirts made up with the logo *Survivors*). In our first year we attended a Thanksgiving dinner given by a group of wives in honor of their husbands. Ten women gathered on the floor of someone's tiny apartment and spread out freaky food — the face mask people were in charge of the diet — on a raggedy blanket. My sister and I were disgusted, both by the ridiculously un-Thanksgiving-like raw vegetables and mushed grain concoctions, and by the facemask people's two boys, who kept opening the door of the bathroom while one of us was on the john. I remember escaping into the back yard and returning only when a high-pitched whistle summoned us; then I remember a processional.

The men had all been gone; it was pathology season. They were learning dissection, and had been held up when something went awry. The wives (my sister and I called them that — "wives" and "men") were clustered around the cloth; someone opened the door; the men filed in like straggly soldiers. They looked sick; I knew this. I knew something was wrong, as I knew something was always wrong in Florida.

The abuses in the program may or may not have caused its shutdown; whatever the reason, a few years later it was phased out, a failed experiment. But what I heard stuck with me, the way the inexplicable stains a child like a scar. One of the men began recounting the day's dissection; his wife reached to stop him; he brushed her hand away. We kids sat poking forks into organic cranberry mash and watching the wives exchange sour glances. The day's body had been a twelve-year old boy, a suicide. The pathology teacher, who I can only hope is dead or committed, had — well, I won't repeat what he had done. But the men wanted to, or needed to, or couldn't stop themselves. And so we sat, and blessed some pagan god for our food, and didn't eat, and in the few remaining years of the program's existence there were several suicide attempts, one double murder.

I remember neon signs on the strip behind our duplex, strange lizards, bits of Spanish, and key lime pie. I remember the migrant workers in the field across the street. Bussed into the city stern, they left stooped. We bought star fruit from their wooden stand; sliced crossways, each piece looked like an icon and glowed pale green. I remember waking Christmas morning to a thousand ants because the candy canes on our tree had melted. I remember my blue satin shirt and gold belt; I remember dancing the Bus Stop to "Jive Talkin'" with my best friend Ann. But above all I remember my father's sorrow, his thin hands on the plastic skeleton he brought home to learn the names of bones, and I remember the names, my father's voice mechanical: *femur, tibia, scapula, clavicle*.

Water

Silver

I am estranged from a few of my former lovers, a loss that tastes like nickel on my tongue. Sometimes I miss who they were: their particular jokes, gestures, intelligence. Sometimes I miss who I was: the behavior they inspired in me, the things they made me feel. Sometimes I miss them for considerably less positive reasons, namely a penchant for bittersweet emotional masochism.

Sometimes missing moves beyond memory.

She is not the woman I loved the most. Not the first or the best; not the worst or the missing. Sex between us was confusing. But I loved a certain silver sharpness about her; I loved how it felt when I peered over that edge. I loved her gestures. And I have come to accept, because I have no choice, that my body misses her the most of all.

I believe in melancholia, incorporation, turning loss into flesh. But I also believe that flesh chooses what to mourn. For whatever reason, my body chose to incorporate her gestures into its own collection, so that now I remind myself of her the most when I feel most myself. The way I talk with my hands comes from her; the way I dance in bars where boys touch boys, shimmering, dressy. The sway of her hands when she shook her hips, out of tempo even with each other. She had an awkward, endearing walk; I've adopted that too, though less completely, given, as I have been told, that I have my own odd walk, involving a kind of piston-strike, straight, with immobile hips. But she was a little pigeon-toed; at times when I feel myself like her — girlish, coltish, awkward but smart — I find myself stumbling in a gait unnatural to me, imitating her, my body grown smarter than memory, reminding me. Because I have incorporated her, I cannot shake her. Gestures remain, the body's calendar, ritual reminders of her and who I was with her.

Begin at the beginning is poor advice for the storyteller. If every life is a multitude of lives lived, lost, unchosen, which life should the writer choose to reveal? To trust in any one voice suggests that this voice — with its particular slang, cadences, concerns — is the self's true witness.

But what if there's more than one self, and several witnesses?

How to tell a truth that shifts?

I think of the woman I lost, the silver lover whose walk is all I have left. I think of loss, of the child I might've chosen, and I believe in mothering, and I am a different person.

How can I tell my story if it changes with the light?

I am not accustomed to the way the sky in Washington affects my moods. Sometimes the blue-black of early morning never changes. Because time is not divided into dark and light, I find myself strangely anticipatory in this landscape, waiting for times of day that never come. Sometimes anticipation is pleasurable; the sky is my lover and I wait for her to silver over. Often it feels more like amnesia than anticipation.

I must learn to incorporate my sun.

In Japan, women lay small shoes, tiny jackets, and miniature hats at the base of a shrine for children-who-would-have-been. Neither penance nor celebration, the ritual is simply an acknowledgment of the loss inherent in choice — any choice. For there might be another shrine for women who have chosen children, a shrine at which books, microscopes, and clocks rest in memory of every mother's unlived lives.

After my abortion, I did not feel guilty or in need of a paternal Christian God's guiding hand. What I did need was a socially acceptable, public ritual to acknowledge the loss implicit in my choice. Rhetoric that denies women the right to choose also seeks to deny them grief that is distinct from guilt.

Solace came in the sound of a voice: a fictitious character named Rose Hobble. At seventeen, she was a high school senior, once popular but ostracized when she became pregnant. Rose spoke to me from a sprawl on the bathroom floor, having just given birth to an infant she never wanted, never even having acknowledged to herself that she was pregnant:

And I bared the cord to the sharp strip that helped and the white bowl and my own hands. And Swimmie sang and the music stopped and everyone listened. We forgive roses. We love roses in winter in winter in winter when the sky is pewter and the snow throws stones. Like water and only one thing sharp a metal I borrowed from the wall dangling Swimmie like time like water Swimmie gouged color on my legs till dark was clouds dark red clouds nimbus clouds with faces stuck in them staining my thighs where he lay to whisper *lost I am and you shall find me.*

I knelt and prayed and slivered that one small thing and then I was whole again.

Red roses for Hobble.

Blood my bouquet.

I came to Rose with my hands cupped, holding time. She whispered to me; I bent to listen. In her story I heard many women's. I think of Suzanne Paola's poems honoring an unborn child's bardo and imagine the child I could've had, hovering. But instead of being tempted by a thousand incarnations, she is knocking and knocking, refused at every door. Finally a panther — sleek, clever — attracts her. But transported into the world of the flesh, the panther is child-sized, a child's drawing of a great cat, manageably small, with a crooked tail and miniature claws. Maybe my cat, Sylvie Sophie, is the bratty kid who might've been. She is aggressive, keen-witted, quick to defensive anger — like me. And she is black, a black cat, which for me means good luck.

Blue

I am lying on a woman's bed beneath an unfinished headboard: a long, narrow birch branch bound with silk thread. Curtains flutter; candles flicker. Above me the wood is as thin as a vein. The carpenter has left it knobby, a twig really, so that the headboard becomes an arbor. Beneath it my lover and I celebrate our harvest, drink from the vines, loosen, reel, sleep. At night it twists and erases itself, reappearing each morning, crimson-tinged.

The branch might be olive; I might be a dove. On the walls around us are shadows that might be wings. In the half-light, the ghost-furniture reminds me of its maker: my lover's ex-lover, who abandoned the project long ago.

In the dreamy world of that bedroom, beneath wood that won't straighten, between words that won't save us, we breathe heavily as we touch each other, as we drink each other's blood. All of my senses are heightened. The pink flannel sheets are downy and warm; the candlelight casts hallucinations. I can smell lotion on her skin, and salt, and sesame. Later I will buy a huge bottle of lotion and wear it, as if my own limbs brushing against each other could make up for the loss of a lover.

I can almost taste her — sweat, blood, hair, nails. But I can't, quite. She will not be incorporated. When I think of her, I think of the headboard — sketched plans for something solid, tokens of peace too easily erased. I think of the bitterness of betrayal and anger, and the sense we stole from each other when we were together: the sixth sense, trust. Belief in reality. It is so easy to gaslight somebody. It is so easy to take someone's world away from them, like removing a picture from a wall.

I believe that we all carry within us some sort of soul. Like a fetus, it can grow or wither, depending on what and how we feed it. I don't think of this soul as some deity's gift, but as our own creation, a spark we strike in ourselves and then must stoke. It is so easy to tempt another person's flame to flicker, then watch it waver, casting shadows that are not what they seem.

To have your vision of reality taken away from you damages you irrevocably. And yet someone with the capacity to gaslight you is usually someone you've let close, someone you love enough to allow inside your mind. This is why lovers have the power to disorient each other:

because to love is to open, and to open is to be vulnerable to distortion.

I open to her. I split, allowing her inside. And for a time this is the most beautiful thing, the cleverest. I am proud, prouder, proudest. Finally I have let myself feel the things I have tried to kill, and the feelings flood me, five, six, seven senses overwhelming everything, till my world is Technicolor and I hear even the shyest angels.

I am in an unfamiliar landscape. Love has cast me there without a map. Within her arms, within the walls of her apartment, beneath her gaze I am strange; my surroundings, stranger. Outside, and without her, the world is also unfamiliar. I have just moved to a broken city, ugly and without mercy, full of coded violence and hidden rage. At night people call their children from firecrackers and popguns, from the squirrels they've stoned and the eggs they've cracked, into powder-blue living rooms where a television holds court like a father asleep, a beer can between his thighs. The girls retreat to their rooms and wait for the incest-curtain to lift. The boys storm to the kitchen, where they badger their mothers for more and more milk.

I am surrounded by children, their eyes purple and grey. They circle my house and knock on my door. Down the block, a women's health clinic walls itself off from repeated attacks; next door, a family of seven spills into the street, children naked or in diapers, their indistinguishable faces dirty and dry, wailing while their parents pray, prostrate before police cars. Nameless, the children throw rocks at my car and threaten to burn down my lover's building. Touching, we cross the street each morning; each morning they keen the same high-pitched dirge. They call us *fags;* they call us *freaks. Spicniggerjew* until one gets it right: *dyke.* Then *which one of you is the man* they question, as they take aim with Coke cans, stones, bent knives.

They are ages seven, eight, four. The eldest is ten, and leads the charge with a baby in her arms, the stroller abandoned in the street.

At night my blue lover and I lie together. I am in her arms, safe in the strange world she's created. At first I like it, like being a character in someone else's novel. Outside her window snow falls, falling faster. We are snowed in. The city sleeps beneath terrible water. I am new to this weather and can't make sense of it. To my eyes, the long flat stretches are ugly; I can smell the stock-yards. The sky favors flavorless colors and whatever season we inhabit wreaks havoc. I am suffocating under the weight of potato chips and pseudo-bagels, ubiquitous stubby brick church fronts, syllabi outdated decades ago. Only the relentless weather — fierce winds, blizzards, droughts, tornados — reflects my inner life, as heat lightning cracks open the heavens, as she takes me beneath a mahogany sky.

Once I see bison silhouetted against a city skyline. Their roughness moves me, and I understand why someone would settle an untameable land.

Once, after a freak October blizzard that knocks out heat and electricity for weeks, I walk through the streets of my neighborhood looking at the wreckage nature has so blithely enacted, admiring its prowess. The autumn trees have not yet shed their foliage; when two feet of wet, thick snow falls in less than twenty-four hours, accompanied by high winds, the trees sag and give in. I walk amidst the maze of boughs bent to kiss over houses and cars, smashing houses and cars; I stumble past uprooted bushes, whole gardens overturned, snow piled in drifts twice my height, drifts green with downed leaves.

Once, as my car rises over a hill, I am blinded by a huge orange something, hurling itself at me with the force of love. I nearly crash as I swerve to avoid the fireball. Then I pull over and perch on my hood, gawking as the harvest moon makes me look small and stupid. My petty life vanishes under the microscope of its fierce stare until I get back in my car and drive on, insignificant and clean.

More often I feel myself in a vacuum. The city is outdated, but also oddly timeless. Strips malls rob me of any sense of distinct community, their long strands of storefronts refusing even the slight solace of a circle. Everything is a chain, useful only as a link to money stored in someone's pocket somewhere else. There is nothing distinct; distinction is feared and persecuted. But at night, in my lover's arms, I inhabit a world so unique I am drowning in its particularity.

I came to the character of Violet by accident. I was sitting on my lover's sofa, trying to explain. All I could think to say was *drowning* though the only water in the city was snow. I felt myself under, under something, beyond my will, beyond my control. I remember loving her fierce gaze, eyes like a hawk's as she watched me gesticulate. But I also hated her coolness, the aloofness that allowed her to analyze me while I spilled over, as if I were a chemical and not her lover.

It was I who used the phrase first: "in the water." Now, estranged, there is no "us." If there is no "us," is there no story? Or do I write to recapture what I've lost or destroyed, or what has been stolen from me?

"I'm in the water," I told her. I, the writer, was unable to think of a more original metaphor. "I've never been the one in the water. Always, I've been dry on shore."

She sat and watched. Her eyes were a hawk's. At night, far away from me, she made love to me, but hid her sex.

I was helpless. I tried, helpless, to tell her I was helpless. I thought I would give up anything; I thought I wanted to. I did want to. I wanted to be helpless, and so I was. She sat and watched. Her eyes were a hawk's. At night, far away from me, she made love to me, but hid her sex.

I wanted to crack her open, as I have wanted, so often, to crack open the stern facades of my butch lovers, women who don rough smirks and stiff collars, whose hands travel my body so beautifully but will not let me touch them.

For a time, I made her a woman.

For a time, she let me touch her, let me show her who she was.

And then she was gone again, and the hawk was back.

I am a woman. I am not a dove. She is not a hawk but a woman, her body motion, her motions liquid, her liquid sheer. The sheer salt of her!

But she is gone, remember.

Keep writing.

Can aggression be tempered with freedom? Can there be an olive branch that is not also a bit?

I made her into prose. I made the salt-sweat taste of her, the damp color of her hair, the sweet tug of her gravity at my hips into a bay, and I called it Ghostwater. A woman walked along its shores every night, seeking her lover's ghost, as I was writing to find mine.

The woman's name was Violet.

Her lover was Rose.

It happened so fast — I was in the water. Blue rose up and I thought I'd drown. Always before, I'd been the one on the island. Standing on shore with my cuffs rolled high.

I'd wave and wave. I'd watch the swimmer and then I'd watch the water. After, if she made it, I'd pat her shoul-

ders with a towel. I'd say, "You're such a fine swimmer."
I'd say, "I can't believe you braved the breakers." She'd
shiver and scuff hot sand. Her hair would dry fast, but her
lips would stay blue.

And her body.

I let both break over me.

I let both salt my lips while my skin stayed dry.

I believed in her beauty.

The water's. The girl's.

I believed she needed to know how to swim.

Shouldn't everyone? Her lips would go pink again.
But changed. Permanently violet beneath the skin.

Violet-on-shore.

Before. That's who I was.

Now there's this difference: blue looks purple and
black. I can feel the sun beneath the water. The grit at the
bottom stings like broken glass.

From shore sometimes I thought *foam sugar*; I thought
release; I thought *ethereal*.

In the water, everything's a bolder color. Gulls swoop
down and flash grey teeth.

From shore I could resist. Tides failed to tempt me.
Gravity droned on without me, pestering seaweed, snails,
gulls.

In the water, tug is constant.

Tug to drown for. Tug to want.

And I want to be here.

And I wish I'd never.

And I wish I'd never known how rough the water.

I see her waving. Not far off but dry enough. I see her
cuffs rolled up, sunburn startling her cheeks.

I see her safety.
I see her ambivalence.
I see her see sea and think it's me.

"You must risk sentimentality," a writing teacher once told me. I have come to agree. It is in sentimental moments that we reveal our most basic and mysterious desires — the desire to live forever, to feel love or passion, to create another being (for what is sweet about that?), to taste someone's sex, to eat and be satisfied.

On starry nights where I live now, the sky is violet and ghosts go knocking. I draw my curtains reluctantly, wondering if I should house them, tempted to believe that the central character of any novel is desire.

Glint

(This is a message to you: not so embed-
ded in the text after all — I could start
now right where we left off.

Talking to you even now, after all this
time. Imagining, after all this time, your
half turn back — that turn that might set
us into animation again.)

Carole Maso, *Aureole*

In Music we are learning to count and to listen. Silver glistens. It tinnies, it tympanies. Triangles gleam, sun
the jewel on each girl's hand. And it is a wedding, wed-

ding of sound and motion, color and company, caution and fire. At twelve, what I know of triangles is the blinding glint that accompanies desire. We stand in rows, girl on girl, curled and peach, lilac and yawning. We stand in rows and strike triangles till silver echoes. From outside, from beyond us, sun wounds our tiny sticks.

I am a listener. My Music teacher doesn't like my voice; who can blame her? It's shrill and squeaky, girly — me. I am all feet and new breasts. My back bleeds where the bra cuts in. *Ting.* I strike the triangle on cue. My best friend does, too. Later, I will stop eating and fade away from her without waving good-bye. I will know I am dying but not try to stop it. I will become accustomed to the sweet smell of hospital corridors, to doing my homework in doctor's offices, to the sounds of the scale — *ting* and *kachunk.* I will keep copious diaries, not of my emotions, but of what I have and haven't eaten. *"You need to get better so you can marry and have children."*

I have lived many lives, most of them triangular. Shifting on the peripheries of vision is my ghost. Not Rose but Kate; Kate, and she is blonde; blonde, and very thin. Long braids down her bony back. She has haunted me for nine years — Kate, dumb blonde. At thirty I turn back, first a half-turn, then full, fecund, Rubenesque. I turn back because I see her — as if suddenly, but with a sense of deja vu.

For a time I believe that the half-turn back is to my lover, a tough saucy butch girl buried in snow. But snow melts, becoming water. Butch girls melt, sweet lips from stone. At thirty I recognize the half-turn back not only as the half-turn back to my blue lover, but as the half-turn back to the self I gave another name before I killed her.

At thirty I realize there has always been a triangle — me, my lover, my old, other self.

In dreams a girl comes to me — enters the bedroom where I sit, bony for twelve, cutting pictures from *Seventeen* magazine. She watches as I rock on the floor, shuffling my butt backwards and forwards, *one hundred, two hundred*, as I press my spine against hardwood and begin sit-ups, my bony back bloody from all I've counted already. The girl watches. She sees the blood on my toes from my pointe shoes, the blood on my back and butt from the hard hands of the wood. She sees the blood caked at my earlobes where my skin flakes and dries to paper. She sees the paper on my pink desk, logs of numbers, calories, miles. Pleasure reduced to onionskin. Thin.

Eating disorders have become cliched in our culture; when we think of anorexia, we think of delicate, shy white girls smiling as they just say no to Little Debbie's and Mallomars. But the reality of anorexia is no Hallmark card.

There was nothing gentle about me. I was always bloody — if not from exercise, simply because my parched skin constantly split open, fire-rose gashes down my hands, breasts, throat — always hostile and cold to everyone around me. I let no one close, not even my other selves. Always in motion, but my motions were never beautiful — I was no sylph, no angel. I was angry. To understand anorexia, you must understand that every pound of flesh, every gash, every sit-up and stoic glance is extracted from spirit.

I don't know what they do for dying girls today, but in my day the treatment was crazy-making. Eighteen years ago I was taught to write: list after list of calories consumed or expended. I was taught girl-math, the math of the fire each bite of food stokes. That was all I knew of passion — the heat of a calorie, the length of a list. I was taught to count. And I was taught to listen — to counselors, doctors, teachers.

I remember few details, but I remember this: what would have cured me was speech. I had lost the language of my girlhood body — the language of solitude, the language of company.

All of my doctors and counselors, and most of my teachers, reinforced conventional modes of feminine behavior. The voices of gay bashers on street corners — "You just need a good fuck" — were predated by my doctors' voices — "You need to get better so you can marry and have children." Now when I hear "You just haven't had the right one" or "You two girls don't have the right equipment" I think of adults assuring me that wellness meant wifehood and maternity. Assuring me that once I was well, I would marry and become my mother.

Over and over I heard talk of who I would become. I imagined losing the surname I've always loved — tall tale and mystery, question mark and command. I tried to feel something for *Smith, Jones,* or *Johnson*, but with *Guess* behind me I balked at the thought. Instead I envisioned my wonderful name lost, a second sock left to wander in a dryer.

No one responded to me as a writer, dancer, student, or human being. I was always a woman — meaning "wife manque" — and yet simultaneously a child who needed to be spoon-fed. No wonder I could not get "well." What was offered up as health was repugnant to me. Long before I understood that I desired women, I understood that I did not desire marriage to a man.

My diaries from this time reflect guilt and turmoil over my artistic ambition, an ambition I saw as selfish and unnatural, even though it felt innate. I wrote of the need to accept permanent loneliness, of realizing I would never love or be loved back. I could not envision a marriage in which my creativity would be understood; I could not imagine a man relating to me as an equal. But without a husband and children, who would love me? I had been taught to be silly and sweet, artificial and demure with men; I had been taught that women — myself included — were not trustworthy or valuable. That female friendship and creativity were childish. That I should let go of my girlfriends, my girlish games, my girlhood. That I should excise what was girlish from my very veins.

None of this felt logical, or even safe. But I was docile, eager to please the adults I depended on for safety, guidance, money — adults I trusted because I had not yet learned not to. So I channelled questions and rage into determined smiles and stoicism. To acknowledge my physical and emotional pain would have meant questioning everything. My world would have caved in. Yet it was the only world I knew.

In ninth grade I was taken out of school and tutored. I was house-bound, not allowed to move too much — a sort of rest cure. And I remember wallpaper — the crazy trellis-pattern of the upstairs bedroom where I'd lie on my back and wait. Wanting speech. Wanting to be either insane or sane, but not halfway, not desperate. I remember the trellis-pattern of the wallpaper the weeks or months (who can say?) I was under house arrest.

So many adults tried to foist on me their vision of femininity. But it is difficult to cure a girl who insists on her own creativity. I wrote scattered poems, kept a secret, second set of feverish diaries, danced at the studio and danced at home. I daydreamed — complicated movie-length fantasies in which I had a voice, and knew how to use it. While my doctors struggled to convince me of the values of conventional heterosexual femininity, I struggled to imagine an alternative.

I was not "sick." But "sick," "crazy," and "mentally ill" were the words used in the hospital, at school, in books to describe me. And so I came to associate illness with art, madness with freedom. In the grand tradition of marriage resistors, midwives, and witches, I realized that to clear the artistic space I craved was to defy convention. While a man who defies convention is ambitious and daring, a woman who defies convention has a mental illness. When male artists talk about madness, they are often represented (like the Romantics) as brooding, mystical, rebellious. Virginia Woolf's despair and Sylvia Plath's anguish came from a different place, and are not glamorous. As Woolf knew, for a woman to crave the luxuries conducive to art — things many white men have taken for granted, such as freedom from child-rearing, time, quiet, solitude, education, artistic community — is to brand herself not only eccentric, but a threat to patriarchal power.

It was easier for my doctors, counselors, and teachers to think of me as crazy than to think of me as having something to protest. If a girl who starves or purges or mutilates herself is "crazy," then our society can go on as it is, not changing, continuing to make young girls crazy while blaming them. *The Yellow Wallpaper* by Charlotte Perkins Gilman intrigues young women today because they know that story intimately: the story in which the victim is blamed, and, just as horribly, in which the woman resists victimization through creativity, but is beaten down until her resistance looks, itself, like craziness.

I remember the trellis-pattern; I remember "insanity." But I also remember wanting to live — more than simply to live, to *be.* I wanted to be significant; I wanted a place in the world; I wanted to make something of my own name. But I lacked models with which to imagine resistance. In school we did not read books by women, learn music by women, view art or movies by women, or discuss women at all except as men's wives, mothers, or mistresses. The women around me were wives and mothers, or wanted to be. I was expected to follow that path. When I found Sylvia Plath's work — on my own, on the sly — I responded to it fiercely, memorizing the late poems, devouring them until my book fell apart in my hands. I understood the need to believe that something I had created would outlast me.

I wanted to tell someone, not just about the terrors I knew, but the beauty. I wanted to describe the ecstasy I felt dancing — the slur of my pointes on a hardwood floor, the speed of pique turns, the gasp of a backbend, the serenade of an arabesque. I wanted to describe the experience of menstruation in a language other than the slang kids used at school. I wanted to make sense of breasts, hips, thighs. I wanted to describe the voices I heard, voices I wrote down then as poetry and now translate into fictional characters.

I heard voices, yes, but I wasn't crazy. My "illness" was protest. I bore within me an activist's passion for truth-telling. I played the family Cassandra; in addition to Kate and Carol, I was Cassie — Cassie who sees too much, and worse, who tells.

When I write, I try to record difficult truths, truths others deny or blind themselves to. I wonder if this is often true of women with eating disorders — if they are activists at heart, women who seek truth in order to foster change. Are we not only our family's soothsayers, but our culture's? And in turn our culture's scapegoats? Seeing and telling; later, conveniently for everybody, punishing ourselves for it.

Recently I have forced myself to look through old photographs. When I see her, that china girl, stick-thin, wistful, desperate, suicidal, I cannot hate her the way I do when I find myself accusing her, believing I asked for it, for everything, for silence and sickness and despair and isolation, for not eating and slitting my wrists and breaking myself by turning pirouettes for hours, over and over, seeking perfection that would kill me or take me away from the terrible things I knew.

"You were beautiful," my sister says. Damaged and silent as I was, my body a boy's, breastless, creaking and bloody. Her voice is a nine-year old's; she too is haunted by a second self. And I see her, one of the few memories I have — I see her at nine, knocking on my door, looking down at me as I sit on the floor. "You are sad," she says simply, reaching out. And I am shocked, shocked that someone has noticed, and I want to comfort her but can't reach back.

I lost her then. We are not close today; who can blame her? My suffering cost my sister her childhood. I think of my abortion, my silver lover's swagger. I think of the girls I teach each semester who avert their eyes and will not speak.

In the dream where, bloody and hopeless, I am trying to carve away whatever weakness, a girl stands over me and touches my shoulder. Touches me with the clarity of an affection born out of hope. Not pity — hope. She sees me. *Turn back.* And she is Carol. In touching Kate I touch myself. The half-turn back becomes a circle. I take her in, that fire-girl. And yet this vision is still hazy; for nine years, I have banished memory.

If I had become pregnant then, I would have killed myself or killed my infant. From this knowledge — ugly, hard-won — came Rose's character, and then Violet, who for a time I hoped could save her lover. But as *Fat Rosie and Rose* evolved, I realized that Rose was dead — she would be. Her impulse was self-destructive; she would kill herself, but let her daughter live. And so the water clasped her, and the fat girl went under, and Violet was left making love to damp sand.

I took pity on Violet, and gave her a living lover to compliment the dead girl. Violet had company; she might've been happy. But she couldn't let go of her past, of her dead. And so she was torn in two directions — between the grey ghost rising from mottled rocks, and the butch girl quietly calling her shots.

✧

My heart is shaped like a shell. Press your ear to my chest and you'll hear the ocean. Love, when it comes to me, comes in pairs — one lover for water and one for dry land.

My name is Violet.

Her name was Rose.

For years after she died, we continued to make love by the skirts of the water. True, her hair was indistinguishable from foam, and her hands, from temperature, but I knew it was her body I'd touched when I woke alone with salt eyes and a mouthful of sand.

With Rose I was always young, a girl, ripe for an unknown future.

Seventeen, and salt. She was part of my body.

She drowned before we had time to know.

It was simplest to go on. Simpler than stopping. Although Rose was dead, she stayed close, so I clung. It was a comfortable triangle. Two girls and a body. A body of water. Water like flesh.

I was a kid when I met Rose. I still believed in happy endings.

Now I'm a woman and believe in ghosts.

Some people cast away the dead and some forget. Some remember with sugar and some taste salt. After Rose's drowning I took a job as groundskeeper at Ghostwater Park. Now I know land as I've known water. I know water as I've known Rose.

I watched them become one. Watched her walk in, over, *on.*

CAROL GUESS *GASLIGHT*   103

Loving Rose, there was no separation. Our bodies blended. No *hers* or *mine.* Without separation, there was no space for desire. Our hungers vanished, leaving Time.

After her death, we made love through the elements. The bay learned to touch me, and the bridge, and spined rocks. Nights, I left the cabin where I lived and walked the same path over and over. I had to remember, or she'd die for good.

I didn't want her to go under, I only wanted her to prove to me and to herself that I could give her more than water.

Instead Rose sank and sank, through blue and then sand, sand and then silt, burrowing under so that when they dredged the bay, they had to do more than dive.

They had to dig.

If Time had wings and could fly over the city of Sehome, it might mistake Ghostwater Park for a tentative smile. That smile nips Ghostwater Bay, which in turn bleeds into the Pacific.

If Time had wings and could've flown over Sehome, I wouldn't be the only witness. I wouldn't be scared of the word *accomplice.* If Time had wings, Time would tell true: how I begged her to stop, how I almost drowned, too.

I remember watching the water's expression change, the way a dog about to bite turns its face to a snarl. When I'm angry at oceans, I try to remember: nothing natural is gentle. The sweetest of kittens turns rose-paws to thorns.

After her death I thought *salt water;* I thought *blue breakers;* I thought *release.* I heard her voice in gulls' cries and sea lace. I heard her voice in my cochlea, as if I were a conch and she was the sea.

WATER : GLINT

I couldn't let go.

Rose wouldn't release me.

Her ghost lodged in my heart's entry. No passing through.

For years after her death I let no one in. I lived alone with Rose's ghost and my anger at oceans. Then Harlan's sharp questions, scratch, my first scotch. A beach towel, folded double. No beach, but water.

I met Rose at noon; I met Harlan at midnight. The difference was visible in the soft flesh at their throats. Suck hard enough on a woman's neck and you taste blood as surely as if you've broken skin. The rose-blush that rises marks her yours for its hours. Harlan's skin was tough, thick and resilient. Rose was delicate, but impossible to mark. I know because I tried, nuzzle-turned-ache. But nothing happened and nothing happened. Her skin was ghostflesh, uncreased and lineless, eerily colorless, untried.

She didn't punish me, Rose, for my night on the towel. She didn't punish me for wanting, or even for fucking.

She punished me for loving.

Yet what's flesh and the commingling of flesh to the arid shimmer of ghost visions and memory? Flesh is dirty. Sweat stings and curdles. Hair crimps the golden surface of your lover's eyes. You have to brush it back, you have to wipe away wetness, you have to apologize later for long, shallow scratches.

"You want to make me a ghost," Harlan said. I had to ask myself if it was true. There's a difference between the dead and the living. The dead are desperate, but the living are blind.

At seventeen, what did I know of *sea?*

The number three is an emotion as much as a shape. Why don't they teach us this in school? I didn't feel the long straight lines, only the sharp angles. Angles and angels. Sharp, spicy, sweet. I believed in Rose's sweetness, though she haunted me. And I believed in Harlan's honesty, though lies spiced her talk.

"You want to make me a ghost," Harlan said.

I had to agree. What could she give me that Rose couldn't? We were sitting on the floor of her apartment, thighs touching, talking of nothing: not dreams, not blue sea. Her statement rose out of nowhere, the way steep waves will. It broke over me, reminding me — not of tides, but river-hunger.

Rivers crave water. More water. Sea.

"You want to make me . . ." Harlan began again, but I stopped her, one palm across her mouth, the other stroking her throat.

Make me, I whispered.

And she did.

She did.

The next morning the water beneath Ghostwater Bridge shimmered, a drowned image shrouded by the surface of the lake. Its dark palimpsest hovered like a negative, first shadow, then shape, then my two lovers' features.

They circled each other like sharks, my silence blood in the water. Three women. A triangle.

How to choose, how to know, how to tell a truth that shifts?

Rust

First, blood. Trail to the body. Along the way cloth-ing: shoes, shorts, one sock. He dragged her by the hair and so there was hair as well; hair, and clumps of more than blood. Skin, nails, bone fragments. Later, a woman who looks exactly like me will hold one of those frag-ments to her eyes and wrinkle her brow.

But that's later. Now — now the police are thump-ing the lot, leaning on pickup trucks and Novas, on a tip from a garbage collector, a marginal man with good vi-sion and the will to see. He came, as he often came, to remove waste, to purify the rusty dumpster so that people could keep on wasting. Wasting away. He came, priest of the suburbs, prostitute of our wasteful desires, and spotted something gold: a necklace. A gold chain.

Serpentine. He spotted something, and then he spotted the body of the girl she had been.

Ghost girl, daughter, grey swimmer who rises from rocks.

No matter her name. This is not her story. Her story is over, shut. She can't read or speak. No matter her name. She is me. She is my lover. This is the dumpster's story, and the asphalt's, and the freeway's. This is the story of the ordinary, left behind.

Several years ago, in a small Midwestern town, I walked my dog past the same rusty dumpster at six each morning. When a teenage girl was raped and mutilated behind that dumpster at 6:03, I stood invisible a hundred feet away. I heard and saw nothing but the ordinary everyday.

Every house you pass on the freeway, every tree, every fence has a life within and behind it.

The quotidian is ominous.

Look at girls' faces.

Look at them.

Sometimes I vanish to an imaginary country. In that fugue state, every girl I see is the girl in the dumpster. Every girl I see is my lover, spread open, a man playing with her body as she played with knives.

Sometimes this vision makes me a good teacher — great, even — the one teacher, female students sometimes say, who has paid attention to them, asked them to speak. *Ever.* They are eighteen, nineteen, twenty-two. "No one has ever listened but you."

Sometimes this makes me a bad teacher, because I want to kill someone and have to cross the room with the awkward gait of a woman who once loved me; open a window and exhale, as if I smoked. Sometimes I want to start smoking then and there, to taste the ash that reminds me of the woman I love — *Blue, where are you?* To welcome smoke as a substitute for angry speech.

Just last week, teaching a student's chapter in a novel-writing workshop, a narrative in which incest is glorified, made "funny" and "sexy," made into a male student's rape fantasy, just last week one of my students, whose own stories chart, over and over, her rape by her father (all of her characters are called *Lepere*), fell asleep but not asleep, fell into a kind of extended trance as the rape fantasy story was discussed in polite, tentative tones as a "clever parody" of porn.

Two female students objected (in delicate, cautious, stammered sentences) to the language of the piece. Both hunched their shoulders forward; they were interrupted by laughter and the world-weary, patronizing voice of a male student who explained to them that they were misreading it, that it was hilarious. That the description of the porn star learning to give head by sucking her father's cock, that her desire to have two men shove their pricks up her ass both at once, her hatred of other female porn stars, how she relegates limp dicks to them — that this was funny.

Realistic.

Ha, ha.

I am thinking about *ha,* how that is not what laughter sounds like. I am thinking about sex, how the women in het porn videos are usually not having it. How whatever magic happens when bodies connect, flesh-to-flesh, spirit-to-spirit, consensual and desirous, wet, beyond innocent, does not glint the same shimmer as shock or coercion.

The young woman deep in fugue tilts her chin to her chest. Her rusty hair envelops her eyes.

I am thinking about speech, about who is authorized to use what forms of discourse. About who pays what price for what choice of words. This student knew his narrative would circulate freely in my classroom; meanwhile, my books are separated out from those of my colleagues at the local bookstore — segregated because of contemporary hierarchies of sexual identity. My books *are* sex because many of the characters are not heterosexual; my student's story is merely *about* sex because it replicates dominant ideas about compulsory heterosexuality and misogyny.

When my colleagues write about sex and gender (and they often do, extremely eloquently), their work is still "literature." If I wrote a novel focusing on lesbian characters in which none of the characters mentioned sex, gender, or sexuality — in which, for example, two women lived together in a relationship but the book centered exclusively on one woman's decision to adopt a child — the book would still be sandwiched between "sex" and "self-help."

Yet this seems to be the book mainstream America wants queer writers to write — books "about" gay people from which any of the specifics of gay, lesbian, bisexual, and transgender experiences have been erased. But could I even write such a novel? How, for example, could I write about a lesbian adopting a child without dealing with the terrible history of queers losing their own children to custody battles? Of queers, well-qualified to parent, who are denied the right to adopt because of their sexual identity? Of partners refused the right to second-parent adoptions? Of grandparents' and ex-spouses' sometimes violent reactions? Of neighbors' questions; of the banal inquiries of people passing on the street?

It is not possible to describe queer life with any authenticity without incorporating the effects of homophobia, heterosexism, and misogyny. Yet to incorporate that kind of necessary material makes a book "political" — and somehow, then, not "literature." How can I respond to the violence of compulsory heterosexuality and misogyny and be taken seriously if my art is always-already marginalized?

Ting.

The telephone is ringing.

In the midst of writing this — thinking about *rust,* thinking about *segregation* — I get a call from a colleague asking me if I can change the time of one of my women's literature classes. A female student is being stalked by her ex-boyfriend. He's attacked her repeatedly, broken into her apartment and methodically slashed her clothing into tiny strips. He's in jail now, but will be out in a few weeks. She is caught in the usual terrible double binds: she wants him to attend batterer's counseling, but for him to do so means he must stay in the area, and she's hoping he'll leave. She wants to feel safe — to live — to know she will live, and so she knows she needs to leave, but her writing projects focus on several female artists painting in this area. If she leaves, she leaves her topic, the people and places she's been reporting on, the publications where she has built up a reputation. To leave is to silence herself. And yet she knows she is in danger.

My colleague clears her throat. Can I change the time of my class so this student will not have to be out after dark? So she can lock herself in her house by six?

I ask what's being done to help her. I'm told she's at the top of the list of women in town marked as potential victims (I didn't know they kept lists. I wonder if I'm on one?), that whoever in whatever position acknowledges that her life is in danger, and that they've given her "the kit." A cell phone and a can of pepper spray.

I change the time of my class willingly. Of course I'll help. Then I can lock myself in at night, too.

I remember Susan Clements, an acquaintance in graduate school. Brilliant, shy, sweet — we used to joke that she was too good a listener because with every other word of a professor's lecture, she'd nod furiously. Susan, who spent one crazy Thanksgiving with her boy-friend, struggling with a half-cooked turkey — a struggle she described with laughter, though she mentioned he was angry, too.

I didn't understand why she moved from an apart-ment on the edge of town back into the graduate dorm. I didn't understand why she vanished from the social scene. And then one morning I woke to a phone call, to someone's voice blurred with tears, to news I didn't be-lieve, even after I heard it on the radio. Susan's boy-friend had driven from California to Indiana with a gun in the trunk. He'd taken the elevator up to her room high in the dorm, knocked on her door, shot her point-blank, shot her new boyfriend, then fled while her dorm neigh-bors, her resident advisor, and her best friend Ann knelt over her dead body in blood and disbelief.

We can lock ourselves in. We can promise het men not to write about the things they've done. We can gas-light other women, mock their experiences, compete with them to fit into a size six — six for the time of day that is both too early and too late to leave the house.

Envy and fear are easier than anger.

Diffuse anger is easier than analysis and political ac-tion.

Don't say it.

Don't write it.

Relax.

How many books would I have produced if self-ha-tred were not constantly taking up part of my mental energy? How many books would I have produced if I'd eaten enough from age twelve to twenty-one to sustain my own concentration? But on some level I was smarter than that. On some level I realized that to concentrate would've meant to see. And seeing — the blood on the rusty dumpster, the nervous curl of Susan's shoulders, my student's shivers — sometimes felt and feels intolerable.

I want to write the book that would've saved me — alerted me, at least, to the existence of women like me. My female students cry in my office not only because they are suffering, but because they believe they are alone. Pain suffered with others, in the company of others, pain suffered with solace, is not the same as pain coupled with the stigma and terror of isolation.

I have long wanted to be alone in a room with another woman, alone with her and not our ghosts. Instead I write poems about a woman I loved years ago whose father haunts me: his ghost always between us, hovering. I never met him. But I know the face he wore when he raped her; I know how he pinned her down. I know what he said because she reenacted the scene with me long before she herself understood.

How my face became his face when I bent to kiss her.

How when she pinned me down, her hands were his.

I didn't want to know what it meant when my silver lover's eyes glazed over, when she shrunk into herself.

Today I call that expression rust. Corroding the sheen of new skin, it eats away unless memory intercedes.

Before I can name my experience, before I can recognize what it means to be pinned down, before I can understand why my lover was so afraid of my gaze, my breath, my hands, my passion, I write poems that tell me, that sit in drawers waiting for me to reread them when I am ready.

My writing self is smarter than my waking self.

Bad Sex

Everything tousled, and then the end zone:
that lie you started things off with
haunts us yet. You shrink from my hands
as I become your father;
the TV flies towards the wall
and I'm wholly new, a violent,
desiring man. Meanwhile, in my reality,
your breasts are in my hands,
we're women overcoming history,
I'm in bliss not wholly new,
violently unaware
that you're not there.

Now you're not here:
two hundred miles by interstate.

I write and call to say I miss
what you don't think we had at all.
But if that's all, whose hands
did I inhabit when I touched
the deer-brown curve of clavicle
that clothed your pulse? Which ghost
pinned both my hands above my head
and bit down hard, trying to reach
its history through my flesh?
I couldn't separate your love
from my discomfort; you couldn't separate
my fierce desire from walking,
evenings, through flooded woods
beside your father. His old brown coat.
Pressing your knee against my throat:
what life in your eyes as you relive
the trip to the river. I just shiver,
liking the perfume of angry breath.

There is a backlash against women who speak up
about misogyny, women who want to document that
part of their history. In order to understand how I became who I am, I need to analyze sexism, heterosexism,
and homophobia; I need to return to passivity and silence; I need to factor in my family's history of enabling
racist violence. These are pieces of the puzzle that is

me. I refuse to give in to, and especially to teach, a literary aesthetic that restricts my access to certain materials and topics. There can be beautiful, lyrical, meaningful poems about rape. There can be beautiful, lyrical, meaningful poems about gays in the military. I refuse to write poems about clouds if clouds are not the puzzle piece I lust to document.

And yet, when I write or teach about rape, abortion, racism, queer sexuality, or violence against women, my work is "political." My colleagues write "literature" while I write . . . What? Political tracts? Trash? When I tell my own truth, the most ordinary sentences become politically charged.

What does it mean for a university to promote "diversity"? In my experience, it means that I am supposed to "be" a woman, "be" a lesbian, without offending anyone. To blend in. I am supposed to "be" diverse — to represent difference — while my straight white colleagues are "normal," and can go on teaching the same way they have been. I (and other "diverse" hires) become a kind of sponge, meant to sop up problematic issues like homosexuality, race, ethnicity, and class, and so allow the rest of the university to have a clean place at the table.

The price for stepping out of line — for going beyond the university's idea of a woman, a lesbian, and "becoming" too feminist, too queer — could be the loss of my vocation. While universities woo "diversity hires," they often do little to retain them. A diversity hire is nothing but a token if she or he is not mentored (profession-ally and socially). The very ideological forces that con-struct people as "diverse" make it difficult for "diverse" people to teach effectively. If I was hired, in part, to com-bat homophobia and sexism, then my university has an obligation to protect me from those forces within its walls. Instead I am expected to battle oppression in class-rooms and faculty meetings while simultaneously suf-fering from its effects. When homophobic and sexist rhetoric is directed against me, my only weapon is of-ten my teaching, which is what is being attacked in the first place. Students argue that my lesbianism "hinders their ability to write." They critique my "feminist agenda" and berate me for being too "opinionated" (white het men teaching the canon presumably are not). I some-times feel I am being evaluated, not on how well I teach (which after all involves enabling debate, friction, and constructive criticism as well as empowerment), but on how well I perform my identities. I am supposed to be a kinder, gentler version of "the lesbian" my students are afraid of.

I have seen this destructive cycle played out over and over again. I have watched universities recruit bril-liant teachers, administrators, and students who in some way represent "diversity;" I have watched these teach-ers, administrators, and students leave campus outraged or shamed because they refused to participate in dis-courses that undermined the changes they were osten-sibly supposed to make. Additionally, the corporatization of the academy has brought with it attacks on academic freedom that are insidiously linked to the rhetoric of "pleasing the customer." This is particularly problematic when it comes to increasing diversity on campus. How can we increase diversity while simultaneously chanting the mantra "The customer is always right"? The "customer" in that sentence is usually a straight white man (real or metaphorical). If he thinks courses in women's literature and queer theory are a waste of everyone's time, is he right? Am I wrong for wanting to teach them?

I am a token, yes, but I am a comfortable token. In many ways I lead a relatively easy life. It has not escaped me that my femme appearance, "white" skin, and class background helped me win this and other jobs. Nonetheless I feel I am a tiger in a cage, looked at, locked in, tamed with fire, when what the university really wants is a pussycat.

Wanting equal opportunities and aesthetic consideration makes me a bad girl — a blood-blot on the ivory tower.

What does it mean for a woman to be silenced? For an academic to be tokenized? For an artist to be ghettoized?

As I developed Violet's character in *Fat Rosie and Rose*, I realized that what made her special — in part because of her lesbian desire — was her outsiderness, which gave her both pain and a vantage point.

She could see.

She could see Rose's belly.

She watched it rise, watched *Rose* become *Fat Rosie.*

I became too involved with my own characters. I fell in love with Violet, with the girl who fell in love with Rose. I wanted Violet to take me away from Rose, from a character too difficult to enter into, too painful. I wanted Violet to take me away from who I'd been — not Carol (whose life seems so comfortable in comparison, whose demons are so well-hidden), but Kate.

I wanted my character to change my past.

And I wanted to write *Fat Rosie* the way I'd written my first four novels: to enter into an imaginary voice, letting that voice carry me far from my own pain. I wanted to invent a woman — like my characters Dell and Peg — onto whom I could project my own despair. Then there would be no shame, only empathy — and indeed I felt empathy for Dell, Scar, Letty, Peg, Jo, Caddie, Tess, Leda, and Helen, for the many characters I've created in whom I can see and empathize with various kinds of terror, anger, miseducation. But I have not been able to see and empathize with that in myself and so have hated myself — Carol, the one character I cannot write.

As I began tracing Violet's connection to Rose, I realized that what I wanted from *Fat Rosie and Rose* —

unlike my first novel, *Seeing Dell*, where I examined a death and a love triangle in a realist mode — was to replicate, not simply the events involved, but the *feeling* of being part of a web. I wanted the reader to feel some of this group's intensity, the slows and starts of their desires. But I failed to capture in print the tug and confusion of having two lovers in a culture that doesn't allow us to express sexual desire for more than one person at a time. I also failed to capture the sensation of going under, drowning with love, feeling utterly out of control in and because of passion.

Rebecca Brown's *The Terrible Girls* captures the feeling of being gaslighted with razor-edge accuracy. While the twists she describes are applicable to any relationship, they ring particularly true to a damaging emotional dynamic — a kind of merger, a loss of identity and will — that occurs often in lesbian relationships. I think of some of Brown's creations — the coffee-cart girl and the bronzed arm. Lesbians steal from each other, steal each other's souls in the name of intimacy. Obviously this is not because we are lesbian, but because we are socialized to become (we are not born) women. That socialization cripples us in ways that increase exponentially when two women face whatever permutations of misogyny, racism, homophobia, and heterosexism haunt them, both as individuals and as a twosome. Obviously, this isn't our fault. Nonetheless, the dynamic exists, and from it comes a whole host of problems within lesbian communities, problems made worse by women's silence about them (a silence lesbians learn from het culture as a survival strategy): verbal abuse, emotional coercion, alcohol and drug abuse, battering, rape.

In *Fat Rosie and Rose*, I had hoped to emphasize the ugliness of intimacy gone awry, become domination, become servitude. It is such a difficult dynamic to capture because it is all about nuance, splitting hairs, gradations. Like a pearl, it is created slowly, delicately, out of a friction that becomes violence.

Fat Rosie took on a life of its own. As I struggled to write it, to write my way through it, it collapsed, red flag after red flag. Storm warning. It collapsed, hurricane. My speech vanished; words evaporated; I was reduced to a stammer; nothing I wrote made sense. The book became a child's rhyme, an extended pun, babble and spit. I could not admit to myself that I was stalled because I did and did not want to tell my own story, did and did not have empathy for Rose, Violet, Coach, and Harlan, did and did not feel brave enough to write a story in which they were not to blame.

The following chapter is all about stammer. It is an attempt to enter into the emotional state I remember, yet to see that state from outside it. When I let Rose die and remain silent, and entered Violet, I hoped that Violet would do what none of my previous characters had done — be both outside my experience, and therefore safe (as Dell, Caddie, and the others had all been removed enough from me to write them), and yet simultaneously inside it, as Rose was meant to be. I wanted Violet to be the in-between, in and out, part and no part, loving and loathing, girl and woman.

Look at girls' faces.

Look at them.

What I remember of swimming the bay: her mouth underwater, mouthing his name. I floated inches away, watching her face through salt's distortions, my eyes burning, both of us burning, me waiting to be breathing again, Rose ready to stop. I tried reading Rose's lips, but grit clouded the syllables. All I could hear was my own held breath. No one knew his name except the bay. It held her secret for her, as I held her secrets, both of us believing if we lied for her, she'd stay.

When you lose someone, you lose a language — thoughts, gestures, expressions created as *we.* There are things I can't know, now; words I can't translate. There are postures, now useless, that once signaled passion; jokes I can't tell; meaningless lines on the ceiling.

When you lose someone in the ordinary fashion, memory replaces the language you've lost. At first memory seems static, dead as the deceased. But memory mutates until it's able to speak.

That language, the language of old self to new, accents the language of your everyday.

When you lose someone in the ordinary way.

But when you lose someone who returns to remind you?

We swim often and late. Late late she's beautiful, shimmer-silver and blue. When moonlight hits her, even if it's tinted gold, her translucent skin absorbs it, darkening it, deepening the fragile pale color of light to something more substantial. I can touch her and feel the scritter of things she knows now.

There are places Rose goes as a ghost that I can't ever follow. Unless I agree:

come with me

come with me.

It's all or nothing. We have this small thing, this meeting — late late and often, gold moon, silver sand — but our real life together hovers just out of reach. It's so big, the decision she wants me to make. Sometimes I try to get her to talk about it — pragmatic, the way I've become.

"Rose," I say to the dead girl, my lover, "Rose, I don't know what it's like. Tell me things. Tell me stories." I want specifics. What's breakfast? What's play? What's death, and how would it feel to go under and stay? I want to know so I can choose. But instead of answering, or even trying, Rose laughs silently, sputter-water; laughs, and splashes my nakedness, which looks different from hers. Laughs, splashes, till my chilly body feels like the corpse of my smart self — Violet Reason. I let go of my talk then, and try to be Star.

We tousle. We rock. We wrestle and suck and touch the parts of our bodies that still nestle gently. Her body isn't what it used to be. There's sharpness where there once was softness, softness where she used to stretch. She doesn't look quite like Rose; she's fuzzy around the edges. She says, using her hands, that I look different, too.

Once in awhile I feel far from Rose, strange and afraid. There's something in her ghost-flesh that feels to me like her old lies. There's a falseness, a silence. I step backwards, towards my cabin, but she always senses it, and tugs my hair.

If I cut it, would I be sorry? Would she reach to tug, and find no rope?

If I let go of Rose, would part of me go under?

Come with and suicide; *let go* and drown.

She's pressuring me, night and day, late late and morning. I feel her breath on my chin; I feel her within me. I miss what we had when we were both human.

What does it mean to be left behind?

For me, on shore. For Rose, in the water.

Funny to think it — once, I was the swimmer.

I came to women as I came to water.

I came to water because of Rose.

Our story's pretty, until you get to her pregnancy. Without that, without *Fatty,* we'd still be together. We'd be a fairy tale, baby dykes who found each other. Girls, we were girls, and if I knew his name, well then.

I'd kill him.

It happened so fast — I was in the water. I came to water because of Rose. Junior year at Whatcom High she twisted her shoulder and quit the swim team before State. There was no one to replace her. Coach paced the parking lot, scuffing her sneaks against slit tires.

I was lifting in the weight room. Coach stomped in to put her team through their paces. Everyone groaned but I just lifted harder, better than her swimmers, who stared like they knew. I ignored them, and sat near Coach when it was time to stretch. With my legs long in front of me I bent forward and held, past the thirty second mark, imagining water so fiercely I made her see blue.

When I came up for air she was holding her breath. "You," she said. "Tryouts at three."

She dropped me in. At first it was too blue to breathe. Too wet; too bloody. Then I turned into a fish.

She liked to watch me. I liked becoming what she saw. I broke sheets of glass into crystal, blinding the turtles, blinding the gods.

Right off, without words, we recognized each other. I swallowed Coach's secret like sputter-water. She saw inside me, past blue, to the flicker-light that said *I am.* Since fifteen. Since Missy. Since a creaky hammock, her parents' beach house, Lummi Island after dark. *I am,* the light said. But I knew to keep quiet. That was part of the knowing, knowing when to shut down.

Her secret. My glowing.

My swimming — fast, flicker.

Won State. Placed Nationals.

Saved the team; saved Rose's skin.

We met in the cafeteria. I was carbo-loading for a weekend race when The Crowd brushed past my table on their way to barf up lunch. My name and picture had just appeared in the *Ghostwater Reporter* because I'd broken the record for the four hundred fly.

"Great fly, Viola."

"Great butter."

"Great breast."

I picked salt off my pretzels while everyone snickered. As they strolled off I rubbed the grains on my palm. I had a paper cut; when she called my name I thought her voice was pain.

"I'm Rose," she said. "You swim really fast."

"I'm Violet. Viola's an instrument."

"I know the difference." Between music and colors. "Vio*let*," she whispered. She made my name both.

Her eyes were the color of ivy on brick. Her stare swam the slow, patient parts of my body. Pasta drooled off my fork. Milk ran through my fingers. Rose's wrist brushed my shoulders. I watched her walk off.

The walk weaves gradually away from shore. Your knees are dry and then your thighs are covered. The tide swims through you, traveling back to transform sand. Your breasts skim the surface, your flails make noise. Your shoulders float. Waves nick your chin.

The bottom drops.

You start to paddle.

You beg the water to support you because there's nothing else to do.

But water's fickle. Sometimes it rescues swooning swimmers, driving them like driftwood to the sand's small feet. Sometimes it rises to cover you because it can. Salt burns your throat, grit pricks your lips, seaweed tongues tickle as water replaces air.

Jealous element!

That's called drowning.

Sometimes it happens; sometimes you dive.

With your face between the risers, salt dripping, strands clinging to your cheeks, musk-scent and fascination, you go down. And the contractions you feel as it tugs you under, the lure of the rhythms, the sound of its pulse, become a dirge as your body gives in.

Rose invented frustration. Her gaze was amazing. She mazed me with alleys, stop-stairways, dead ends.

In bio lab, with all those doomed mice, I started tracing the maze she'd made from plywood and paste.

What she did next had not been done. While I stared at her beauty, liquid eyes back and back, she led my whole hand through the maze that she'd made. My wrist ached. Started shaking. Teach smiled in our direction. A quick glance at our breasts.

"How're my cheerleaders today?"

Rose was fixing her makeup in the ladies' room. She brushed brown sparkle beneath her brows — a whole new face of crazy colors. Then she checked beneath the stalls.

No shoes.

She dropped a lipstick and the blood stain spread.

It might've happened then. She might've touched me, but the bathroom door opened on Somebody Boney, her lips full of doughnut holes, dying to get rid.

Rose turned the other cheek, streaking it cinnamon. Bones barfed sugar while I shook the machine.

Lesson girls don't learn in History: good cotton-pickers plug their holes.

I unwound the tampon, searching for my fortune. At the center was more cotton, dyed white to bleach my blood. They say the bleach seeps into women's skin. They say the bleach is toxic. They say

be pure
don't leak.

Bones wiped the vomit from her powdered cheeks.

Exeunt.

Exhale.

It might've happened then.

I dropped to my knees to congratulate crimson. Licked her broken,

lucky
lucky

stick. It might've happened then — she might've touched me — but the door opened on summer and Rose was gone.

✧

All those long hot months I dreamed of lying. I lied to my folks about lying on top. And dreamed of lips. And dreamed of softball. But not of Missy, who bored me, though I'd once said *don't stop.*

I watched her swim and then I watched the water. After, I patted Missy's shoulders with a towel. "You're such a fine swimmer," I said, meaning *loser.* Meaning *I'm dry, you're drowning.* Meaning *I'll write the ending.*

And the ending was Rose.

Nibbling toast in a mansion. 212 Surgeon Circle, near VP Way and Lawyer Lane. I'd ride out on my bike, my cap tucked low, my body hidden beneath a baggy shirt. I didn't want her to see me if she happened to step out.

But she never stepped out.

She played indoor games.

Light B&D. Ecstasy. Wine coolers and coke.

I stayed mostly clean and hung mostly with Missy, who parted her legs and stayed wet all day. She'd mark up my neck while I dreamed about Rose and lied to the rents about the rash on my body.

"Poison ivy," I'd say. My parents believed me. I watched Missy miss me while my cuffs stayed dry and my heart stayed sandy. At night I'd stretch a long slow press against my mattress, imagining that I was brick and Rose was ivy.

A long, slow climb.

When I licked her lipstick from the pink tiled squares? I thought *down down* or maybe *drown drown;* I smeared my face with her fakeness; I tasted the simulacrum of her lips.

I tasted patience.

And Kendoll took her hand. And she kissed him in front of her locker, which was decorated with pictures of Leonardo DiCaprio. And the boat sank. And I went under. No room on the lifeboats for girls in top hats.

She kissed him hard; he pressed his prick against her belly. Then he stomped off. Football-year Chemistry.

And I turned away and it was over except that for a second there, I thought she winked.

I turned around, expecting salt.

Rose stood ashimmer.

The hallway stretched like senior year. At the long length's end the window winked. But what was weather and what was human temperature? If she kissed my lips, I'd just taste his.

She brushed close, then closer. Softness. Sugar. Things he wanted from her. Things I could give her.

"You swim really fast."

"There's him."

"He's slow."

"Someone might see."

"Two girls together?" She was laughing, gritty. And I was scared, as I should be.

It happened so fast — I was in the water. Blue rose up and I thought I'd drown. Always before, I'd been the one on the island. Standing on shore with my cuffs rolled high.

From shore I could resist. Tides failed to tempt me. Gravity droned on without me, pestering seaweed, gulls, conch.

I saw Rose waving. Not far off but dry enough. I saw her cuffs rolled up, sunburn startling her cheeks.

I saw her safety.

I saw her ambivalence.

My heart turned to water, wave on wavelet.

Poor, soggy Violet!

I drowned inside before my head bobbed under: once, twice, the third time the clincher.

When I came up for air, Rose was straddling my shoulders.

"It's just *practice,*" she said. And so we were *practicing* when Rose forgot her name and tugged out her own hair. When she leaned into me hard and then harder, eager, spreading her fingers, finding my pulse in unlikely plush places, when she made cries caused by my lull-to-liquidity, my conch-uncoiled stretch, still, still we were *practicing.*

She went to college parties at the U. Frats and such. Small cuts along her inner thighs.

I began to miss her when we weren't together. I'd never missed a girl, though girls had missed me. They'd described their misery while I listened, lips taut. I felt envy, not empathy. I wanted to crave somebody. But sex stopped at the point where the breakers began.

Then Rose. Knew me. I knew when she touched me. I knew there was somewhere beyond where I'd been.

Soon it slipped out — the word *love*, like a hiccup. Rose

flipped

her hair. "It's just *practice*," she said.

Kendoll was human. Pink flesh and *bone*. I was just water. Sea foam and *spume*. So she hid me inside her. Eight glasses a day. Water for beauty. Water for play.

Now I was struggling, arms thick and heavy. The water went on, as when a lover won't come. I couldn't see shore, only glints on the water, the water my trial, its dazzle undone.

Sex with Rose was Science — I learned about gravity. The tug that refuses to listen to *slow*. I remembered what Coach said — cross training's a hoax. You train for a sport by repeating its motions

over and over

two fingers inside her. My shoulder blades burned and my fingers went numb. She was slow. I was simple. I'd come

Snap!

and my surname

Star.

No one at school ever guessed we were lovers. If they had, who'd have guessed she liked lying on top?

Who'd have guessed she was difficult, while my body unravelled?

I was drowned and on fire — the worst of both elements.

I discovered this in increments.

Is it always a cycle? The taker is taken. We give and we get and we die in a box. Do we teach when we steal? Is the lesson a gift? Is the lesson we've given worth more than our theft?

There are strokes that say *bind me.* There are strokes that say *dear.* There are strokes that leave stripes that mean nothing but *feel.* Sensation. The writhing. The reaching for something. How can sex be about love when it's first about motion?

She'd kiss me, lips tight, till I asked, "What's the matter?"

"Nothing." More "Nothing." And her focus was gone.

Once, after "nothing," I rode my bike home. Past neat rows of houses with subtly trimmed doors. I wanted the key to those sweet, well-lit houses. I wanted to know how they'd come to be homes. I couldn't imagine a house of my own, or a girl who would love me for more than the time that it took her to come.

Missy said she loved me. But I couldn't remember
the color of her pupils
the lines on her hands.
I held Missy's heart away from her body
the pulse-flag
of a country
women weave with their mouths.

I stole Missy's stories. They became mine or Rose's. I was always afraid I'd call out the wrong name.

Someday Rose will miss me — Violet Star. She'll call out my name in the backseat of his car. She'll try to forget but my name's shape will haunt her. She'll see stars and remember several triangles together.

Someday Rose will miss me. She'll learn to spell loyalty but by then there'll be babies. Never for me. I won't split myself open. I won't pause my own life to jumpstart a new one.

I know how she'll walk. She'll trail-cloud her veil. He'll smirk as he lifts it. Her lips will be pale. And they'll sing holy wholly; they'll sing Virgin Mary. They'll sing and they'll clap and gift wrap Mr. Coffee.

Silver paper.

Gold rings.

Violet stars on her gown.

She'll summon amnesia — Godmother, come down — and sing hymns at Christmas. Bake chocolate chip cookies. Learn to make oatmeal and sweaters and time
  for his hands and his habits
  for Junior and Sis
  for soap operas and cufflinks and Mr. and Mrs.

Rose also hurt Rose. She knew that she missed me. I can still see the cling marks etched into my body. She looked to be clinging. The real motion was climbing, her lips little balloons. She'd push me away. I'd go back and be humbled. The very next day. I went back. It was true. I couldn't give up

the rose slide into blue

in the font of my mouth. She held open her palms. Let me drink from her nails.

She liked girls more, in general.

I knew this. *I knew her.* At the cock's toodle-loo —

"Don't tell" —

she denied me —

"or I'll hurt you, too."

Hurt who?

As if *hurt* had a tempo; as if it waited for tell. She'd already hurt me. She'd touched my whole body with a tongue that told lies and two hands that stretched truth.

Kendoll wanted a bimbo. A doll-hole for his pleasure. He'd aim, always miss her. She'd come to me covered with dried crusted sorrow; I'd lick away salt till she was pink, silky, new.

Then she'd stop coming. She'd vanish within him. I wouldn't see her for days; in school she'd ignore me.

I missed sex with Rose every time we stopped fucking. But I'd missed sex with Rose before our first kiss. To miss something for real is to miss its existence even before you know what it is.

I tried making up. For awhile I ate cookies. Ginger and frosted. Butter and chip. But my tongue knew the difference between *lover* and *friend*. Crazy. I felt crazy. I missed sex with Rose the way I knew I'd miss living when I was dead in my grave.

Grave and no-go. *Grave* my dry body. When she went off with Kendoll, water left me. No crying. No tears, just
sweet silver clouds hanging low over my body,
clouds I could touch if I stood on my toes. But I was never a dancer; that was Rose. Later, as *Fatty,* Rose quit that too. Tossed her pointes in the ladies'. I saw one peep out like a girl's wave good-bye to the body she'd loved, knowing breasts would soon dull her. Knowing blood would soon drag her whole center

low

down

The

on Rose was that boys were her forte. This was her weak spot. The reason she feared me was that I'd blab our secret. The secret of *fucking*
girl hands on girl knees.
When I got hungry she punished me. *Over and over.* Yet there was something between us I won't find again. I don't have to remember. My body relives
what was wet, what was dry
the tug of high tide.
So we'd return to our coupling, though cautious, though tired.
I tried not to love her.
My heart came back proud, but my body. *My body* was desperate *again.*
She looked me hard on. I knew where to take her.
I loved it in bed — the harshness, the teeth.

I loved when she climbed me.

Loved when I bled.

I loved when she took me, my hands on her head. When she pinned my wrists down. I never learned what she said.

To Kendoll.

To others.

Greek letters.

Warm beer.

I was only the *girlfriend.*

Not *father.* Not *husband.*

Not the grown man who owned her on Wednesdays and weekends.

They never spoke, and yet his touch turned her whole life. He'd wait till the baby was sleeping and then shake open her legs like *The New York Times.*

His face looked like a reader's.

He'd mutter and mumble.

He'd shuffle and page and then finally *recycle.*

When she told me, she was drunk. It came out of her mouth like a child's tooth, bloody and unexpected.

"What?" I asked. I thought I'd misheard her.

He was ten years older. She baby-sat his daughter.

No adults anywhere. There never are.

Girls teach themselves and each other masochism so Big Men won't kill them. "I'd rather be raped than dead," Rose said.

Now, if someone laughs and says
you're so emotional you made this up this isn't true
I say
prove
what you're saying
go
to a classroom
look
at girls' faces.
Look at them.

I swam into the storm.

Lightning skirted the water. All around me were flares pointing silver to shore.

Sand crackled with static; foam fanned into flickers. Blue sparks seared the water, singeing my hair.

The ocean was boiling. I stroked through the glitter. When I glanced at my arms, they glowed peach in the dark. I carried it with me — the storm's electricity. When the thunder died down my skin tingled and shone.

The things that Rose felt, she felt full force and hard. Whatever she felt, she drove on with that feeling. When it was done, she'd stand shaking her head.

How did this happen?

What was it I said?

She looked like a cheerleader after a binge: fingers touching her lips, eyes astonished, mouth open.

She couldn't believe that she'd eaten the thing.

She couldn't believe what she'd given away.

Rose would drift into trances. Not slowed-down and sluggish but speeded way high. Her gestures would widen, her voice pick up. Huge things happened quickly. And then she was sorry. She seemed very present; in truth she was gone. Her body took over. Her mouth carried on.

Time after a trance was spent picking up pieces. Repairing the weave of the fabric she'd torn.

Rose would carve bits of new flesh from her body.

Rose would caress anybody she'd snubbed.

Sometimes it was me.

She said *sorry* with kisses so often I'd come to see *sorry* as sexy.

To feel sorry for sexy.

To feel sorry for Rose

when *Rose*

hurt *me.*

The trances felt old.

I wanted presence.

What she had with her*self.*

Rose loved Rose.

There was nobody else.

When presence was gone we were statues.

Stone.

Rose faked she'd forgotten our *mutual moans.*

Then more sorry, with kisses, so often I'd see

S

in her body's slack shape on the floor,

O
in her smirk.
But the *Y*
came from me.
Why?
Why me?
Why Rose?
Why him?
The father. The husband.
He paid baby-sitters $6.10 an hour.
Once, she and I had a long conversation about how much she'd get if she called herself *whore.*
"I ought to be paid for it."
We read books about prostitutes.
We learned what girls learn to make sense of their world.

In school they made us memorize our fathers' names. Over and over: Dickinson, Morrison, Winterson. And their occupations: Archer, Taylor, Jon. Our mothers vanished. Only in the lunchroom could we smell their hands.
Mayonnaise. Molasses. Mustard and milk.

Kendoll dumped Rose at the start of the semester. The Crowd acted edgy with her, after that.
Damaged goods.

WATER : RUST

For awhile she made up for it. Frat parties, the usual. Then the fatness fell, things got worse, finally impossible. It was The Crowd's deepest fear. To be *Fat* was to suffer. To be cast into the hole that was Being Unpopular. Kendoll brushed past her as if she was a locker. And maybe she was; maybe I had the key.

Her named changed. From Rose to

Fat Rosie

and I were still lovers, sort of, though she barely let me touch her. She'd tear into me, hungry, then recoil from my hands.

I didn't understand.

We were at her parents' house; I think her parents were out. We'd locked the door to her room and turned on a CD. Her hair stained the pillow, some dark color — it was always changing. I ran my palm from her forehead to her throat to her chest and then down, over the slight curve of her belly, till Rose pulled away.

"Don't," she said, and then she was crying.

I watched, not speaking, barely breathing, tasting salt. "Don't hurt yourself, Rose."

She didn't know simple things, like drying her eyes *tenderly*.

The problem was her parents' money.

The house was noisy, staticky with crisp new bills. Her mother was silk, boneless like a cat. Her father was the sound of cufflinks fastened on by someone dark. They were surgeons, programmers, art dealers, or gamblers. They were rich, for certain, and should not have had children.

As Rose became *Fatty,* as she lost her slot in The Crowd's hierarchy, she turned more to herself. Beyond merely autonomous; more like self-adulterous.

Her belly grew rings like a tree stump or target.

Kendoll threw pencils and scored.

I watched the public crucifixion — her outstretched arms sagging beneath the weight of a lunch tray.

And the private mutilation — her nipples' stigmata.

When I reached for her, she pulled away.

I didn't like who I was almost all of the time. Only swimming released me — from *Violet,* from *Rose.* It stopped being for drowning. Now dry land felt worse.

Coach helped me get through. The other teachers were toxic. I'd drop by her office, my hair stuck to my nape. Sometimes my thongs squeaked.

Water. Wet *glicks.*

She'd stand during practice, dry on the edge, shading her eyes from the clerestory, pursing her lips in a straight blue line.

Thin, that line.

Between *muse* and *water.*

Between *water* and *lover.*

I knew I'd miss her. In a year I'd be gone. To one of those colleges where tomboys are *strong.*

I'd miss what she taught.

Not breaststroke.

Not fly.

The *why*

of the *wanting*

what's wet

or what's dry.

Our real lover is Time. Her sure hands never falter. She flips us; she tops us. And then she moves on.

I threw myself into the water.

Coach read my grief in the shapes that I lapped.

She knew not to ask. She knew not to bother. I turned glass into water, water to speed.

I watched Coach watch the team weave laps over and over. She stayed dry. She stayed sandy. I saw her cuffs rolled up, sunburn startling her cheeks.

What kind of a swim coach won't swim?

She was young, Coach. Twenty-five, thereabouts. I wanted to ask what had happened to beach her.

But I just swam faster. And the rains held back. And I felt Rose's belly rise, tighten, and shirr beneath the palms of my hands as I bared my throat to lick her.

Drizzle

There is a kind of rain here that doesn't leave marks. Halfway between wet and dry, it falls but doesn't stick — breath more than water, more beautiful than sun, and tangible. I like drizzle, fog, mist; I like tangible weather. Whatever color the sky, I walk by Bellingham Bay often, and alone. Even on the bleakest, drizzliest December mornings, weather tourists complain is dull and sloppy, I find in the echo of dark on dark or light on dark tints I have never seen anywhere else in this country. The South I remember was lush, but that lushness was tropical — there was orange in it, and every kind of pastel. Here everything comes from and returns to blue: violet, cerulean, indigo, and sometimes steel, the bay's surface dazzle-drizzled pewter. Hard blue is my favorite color. I cannot believe my luck — to live in a landscape where everything comes from and returns to the tint my body misses.

On a walk I take often, there is a wooden bench that stretches longer than I am tall. Its metal uprights are shaped like people, and I greet them as I go. The path curves for a short while along a busy road, full of Fairhaven shoppers gawking at the view of the bay that drops off, steep, to the right. On the left are honeycombed condominiums, each with their own hundred thousand dollar picture window. I imagine how small the bay would feel, seen through a square whose shape never changes. It is not enough that the light be different. There must be motion for me to see something; I must be in motion; I must be leaving, or coming home.

My family moved often, and seriously. None of those "across town" or "down the street" moves for my family. While each state and city remains distinct to me, I have no memory of the in-between. I've come to realize that I have no memory of transitions because, after the first several moves, transition became being. I am used to movement, to instability. There's stability in it for me. I am made of impermanence.

I remember a game we played in graduate school, silly but telling, as games often are. Someone with a thesis to write decided that we should come up with a nickname for every creative writer in the program. Rather than use the imaginative portion of our brains, we decided to rely on stereotypes, and picked the name of a country for everyone, based on generic associations: Italy was passionate, England aristocratic, America tacky but enthusiastic, etc.

When I found out I was Ireland, I breathed a sigh of relief. Lush green landscapes — surely this was a reference to my deliciously lyrical writing style? Pretty soon I garnered no. Over a few beers it was explained to me in gusts of hilarity that I was Ireland because I was always two incompatible halves.

What struck me then, and still strikes me, was how folks I didn't know very well could see this in me: my doubleness, my split. The woman who coined my nickname knew me only tangentially, yet she'd picked it, and everyone else nodded in agreement. It was one of those moments you remember, not because you were hurt or pleased, but simply because someone held a mirror to your face and forced you to see yourself seeing yourself. I had not realized I was so transparently what I was.

"You're all one thing, then you're another. You're whatever you are very hard and stubborn, until five minutes later you're another thing very hard, and so on." The table nodded like one body. I was reminded, gently, of my penchant for hyperbole — everything that happens to me is *worst* or *best*.

Part of me is proud of this. I like my energy, my passion for whatever I've found to be passionate about. Over the years, I've tried to train myself to take that energy and direct it towards useful, or at least ethical, pursuits. The more of it I channel into my writing, the better. What

I feel, I feel full-force and hard. Something good feels, in that moment, like the best thing. Something bad feels like the worst — intolerable, impossible to bear.

Sometimes I think I experience time differently than the people around me. Things seem to move slower; I am always pushing for the speeding-up. Once my blue lover pressed her ear to my heart and told me that my clock was so because of my pulse.

My resilient heart beats very slowly.

I like things to happen quickly.

Then to make messes, find complexity again.

From this temperament comes a fascination with greyness, with the in-between. I don't understand moderation. Even as a tiny girl, I was where and what I was as hard as I am now: when I was playing some crazy kid game, I became the character and stopped being Carol. My friend Meg and I used to play witches, and when we were witches, the world fell away.

I dislike flaccidness. I dislike limp handshakes, vague smiles, small talk, acquaintances. I have several best friends, and then I have enemies. Or rather, I have best friends, and then there is scenery. If I don't like someone enough to love them, they cease to exist, they are not there.

I don't recommend this as a way of being in the world. But on the other hand, the typicality, in American culture, of benign politeness, of "friendship" based around casual conversation and geographical proximity, makes no sense to me. I cannot stand to spend more than ten minutes with someone if our conversation isn't going to scratch some surface. Just as I think of myself as having gaydar, so too I like to think I have a kind of friendship radar that trembles when I sense, in someone else, the potential for depth. In this way I am Dell, the dead girl in my first novel, the one who couldn't stand parties because she couldn't make small talk even if she tried. When I open my mouth, I say what I'm feeling — the rough, sticky things, the passionate things, the beautiful and the cold. My friend Nichola likes this in me; she says I'm one of the few people she knows who mean it when I ask, "How are you?"

Why ask if you don't want to know?

As a graduate student, I had trouble making sense of academic coolness, of the vague nod in the hallway that passed for a greeting (I mistook it for a tic), of studied politeness, of acquaintances that, like alleys, led to bricks and more bricks. I've learned well since then the smooth smiles, the bordered conversations — English gardens pruned well, and often. I do not bring up inappropriate topics of conversation. I smile, I say I feel well, I distinguish collegiality from honesty and intimacy.

But my students weep in my office all the time. They come out to me, they write about being raped, they grapple with death, eating disorders, miscarriages, their parents' divorces. They tell me they feel things. They bring me pictures they've drawn to go with our readings. They laugh in class. They read their writing. Sometimes they dance, or draw pictures in chalk. I love my students because they are raw, like me. And I try to tell them, through the veil of academic distancing, that I understand rawness, and value it.

I've long believed that my penchant for extremes comes from growing up with the mother and father I was given. They are wonderful people, married over thirty years and still in love. But as a child I found them confusing models — opposites who together formed a whole, but taken separately required entirely different worlds of me. My father is brilliant, a genius even — a mathematician turned physician turned scientist. He began his career helping to invent the nuclear submarine and now invents vaccines. He is serious, my father, mind and more mind. Though he is very handsome, I do not think of him as having a body. He is somber and aloof and distant and cautious. To talk to him is to understand anything, anything at all — anything but intimacy. And yet like me, he makes himself vulnerable very suddenly, unexpectedly, and hard. Like me, he has moments of bizarre goofiness. We both sing to dogs — complicated, sincerely heartfelt songs with many verses. Like me, my father cannot carry a tune.

My mother is all body, all smiles and gracious gestures. She is impossibly pretty, delicate, the essence of a femininity even I, who think of myself as femme, can't imagine achieving. It would take the rest of my life; indeed, it took twenty years, until I gave up in exhaustion. Much of my first two decades were spent pursuing what was, for me, an impossible ideal — stylized femininity, sleek and demure.

My mother is body to me. But she is also intimacy, and yet not really. She is beloved by her students in the Wives' Club at the local university, sent to her to study ESL. They adore her, write her letters calling her an angel, telling her how much they miss her. She is an excellent teacher, my mother, but she teaches out of her home. To preside over a classroom would be to occupy the public sphere—to ask publicly for recognition. My mother has reading groups and lunches, secret ladies' clubs, best friends and acquaintances. She is a gifted artist, able to make of domestic pastimes—quilting, cooking, decorating, dressing—lush, often startling art. She is always tending to someone, a tender Florence Nightingale for the suburbs, while in her visual art she takes fierce, witty risks.

I wanted very much to be her, to be a woman in that way. But I failed at nurturing even myself. In my teens I was much more my father than my mother, much more the distant, dreamy scholar, the forgetful writer who scrawled lines on tablecloths, who drifted away in conversation, never to return. Being more like my father confused me terribly, because, as a woman, I grew up body.

Both women and men in our culture often feel this split, this division between the realms of masculine intellectualism and feminine intimacy. The fact that I am describing each of my parents as representative of one gender category testifies to the impact of sexism and homophobia on their generation, and now on mine. What part of the woman in my father is lost forever? What part of the man in my mother is always invisible? Would knowing that woman, that man have saved me from hating those parts of myself?

I wanted to occupy both of their worlds, but I didn't want them coded "masculine" and "feminine." To me, my father's intelligence had a feminine tinge — a delicacy, a gentleness. And my mother's gorgeous domestic arts had a masculine ambitiousness, an ardor. Recently diagnosed with breast cancer, her pale hair fallen away, she has made of scarf-wearing an intricate, defiant art akin to origami. Feminine, yes; also bold and life-affirming.

Like it or not, I vacillate between becoming my father and becoming my mother. My extremes represent them, and the worlds they inhabit. My closet is divided into boy clothes and girl clothes, butch and femme. So too my gestures, my speech patterns. I associate these realms with the pleasures and dangers of each — the ambition and coldness of masculinity, the intimacy and frivolity of femininity.

This is why I write early in the morning, before the world crashes down on me, before I am dressed and presentable. I write in my bathrobe, not as a professor, activist, or lover, but as sleepy Carol, my dog at my feet, coffee glued to my fingers, the sky outside lush violet-black. In those early hours I am whole, wholly myself. I am mind and body both. My words are an extension of self, not a distraction or a choice.

As the day goes on, I cannot be everyone. I must choose, giving up bits and pieces of a complex whole. Teaching especially requires the winnowing of the self. There is so much of me I cannot, must not, show my students and colleagues. Sometimes I like the self I do show them better than who I am; many shy people go into teaching for exactly this reason. But as a writer and a woman, that cutting off of self from self is damaging. It's what girls learn to do, too often; what Great Men have taught me, what I have had to unlearn.

When I teach writing, should I see students' writing or should I see students? Teaching demands both too much and too little curiosity, as well as a selflessness that does not come easily to a serious artist. As a woman, as a feminist, I feel I have an obligation to answer pedagogical questions differently than male professors of yesterday. It is not enough to stand up and lecture, not enough to remain aloof and dispense knowledge as a doctor dispenses pills.

The character of Coach — the swim coach who becomes a mentor to both Rose and Violet — evolved as a way to examine someone split in two, at war with herself. Through Coach I also began to examine what it means to teach students your particular art — that is, to teach them, not some general field of knowledge, but the precise thing you are struggling with on a daily basis. There's a thrill in it, in sharing secrets, talking through difficulties, exchanging triumphs. But there's also a terrible jealousy as students breeze past whatever records you have set, as they surpass you. Coach doesn't even see her students; all she sees is her beloved element, water. And yet she can't let it embrace her, torn as she is between liquid and a living lover.

To love someone is to let the world narrow to the point that is your partner's heart.

And if your partner is motion?

And if your partner is within you and everyone?

We see each other every day. Mostly we ignore each other, or pretend to. Of course I notice her shifting colors. And of course she tends to the students I send her — caresses them, yes, but teaches hard lessons.

I stand on her rim and gaze out at her body.

She gazes up at me, she lures me, I almost fall.

And it's like sitting over Harlan, using two fingers, blinding her to anything but pleasure.

But better.

I feel her inside me; I feel her against me; I feel her rise over and cover — *become* — me.

Harlan loves me, but she'll never drown. Safety means ambivalence; passion falters without risk.

With water, I love the echo of loss. With depth comes fear; with fear comes value. We crave in each other ways the other wavers.

Still water stagnates. Its skin slicks, poisoning swimmers and multicolored gardens. Moss silences the thousand lips of its undulations. But sea breaks her own surfaces, blue-rose rising. She laps at her borders, altering herself in ways women won't.

Water is process. Water becomes.

Harlan slops soup and stains my silk sheets.

At night I dream of leaving Harlan. But when I wake, she holds my face between her hands and reads me aloud.

The signs are on the surface. The signature of dreams.

For many years I swam, myself my best element. The wetness around me meant less than my skin. I raced and won races. Clocks applauded my skill. Gradually slickness replaced skin, and women were only Not Water — the spaces between splash, the lack of continuity. The clock kept ticking, but their bodies vanished. Instead blue devoured flesh and I let loss become love.

Women remained on the periphery of my vision. I learned to read bodies by watching water change shape. When a woman dives, water coils, then clenches, a violent fist or the memory of light. Like chalk outlines around a wasted body, blue illuminates the past.

At first it was easy to watch the swimmers. I followed their bright skin with my eyes and felt smart. But slowly I realized I was missing their meaning. Water answered my questions. Bodies were only remarks.

When Harlan came along, I thought she'd changed me. I was drawn to the desert of her scent and hair. She smoked, exhaling clouds that dried like froth. Her mouth and lips were parched, coarse like the bottom of a river. I took her everywhere her blood could go. When I stroked her, the space my tongue and hands knew was rough, its ridges swollen to striation. I reached so deep sometimes she'd hold her breath. So deep we both worried she might not come up for air.

Which Harlan loved, as she loved smoke, sand, summer sun.

Her hair combed sparks. She bled in clumps, black-rose clots unwinding in the belly of the bowl. Her body clung to its moisture, doling out sweat and tears like molten gold. When we kissed, I tasted dryness. I was always digging. Her real name vanished in the desert of her throat.

She was younger, Harlan, but old-school in gesture. Her game of pool was impeccable; her drink, house scotch. Surrounded by Rubenesque femmes with delicate features, she'd call her shots quietly, showcasing her wrists.

Harlan's shots were a bachelor's. She hit straight. No gold circles. Then she met me and her aim swung around.

We'd tussle some, each trying to be the first to touch. Touch-test. First, best. Tousled, tense. Still Harlan knew nothing of my love for water. I had my two loves, and my loves loved me.

Harlan, so arid.

Water, so wet.

My landscape was bounded by desert and sea.

I loved being the middle; I loved being both. My mouth was moist; my fingertips, dry.

Then I began to notice signs.

For a time when I met Harlan, her eyes took me while we kissed. I topped her, yes, but her eyes flipped me. I looked deep in and they turned me over, like hands. They turned me over lovingly like hands because they stared me down; they stared me down because she tried to see through me. And, trying, she worked her way inside me.

All that stopped when she turned to jealousy.

Jealousy's not seeing through but walling off. Her eyes stopped trying and started flickering. I'd look at her and she'd look away; when our pupils met, she'd stop her gaze from diving.

She took the easy way out.

She wanted less of me, not more.

She wanted stasis, not easy motion; she wanted our lives to stay exactly the same. And so she tried to freeze the live blood inside of me, to turn what was liquid to ice she could crack.

Back then, at the U, I coached in the water. I gave each day's lesson standing knee-high in blue. And I held a few of them around the middle to show what I meant by this or that stroke; I tugged on their legs, shoulders, arms to fix their form; I showed the difference between splash and slide with my own body.

Across town, Harlan was burning sepia with jealousy.

She never said it. I just knew.

One night she confronted me. When she asked *who* I sputtered and stammered. What to say? It was true. There had always been another partner.

The sea winked sapphire and I swam too far.

"You want to make me a ghost," Harlan said. She talked of live and dead things as if water weren't living. She talked of love as if love was glass — to be fired once, violently, then guarded tenderly its whole stiff life.

I took her favorite vase from the mantel and turned it around and around in my hands. The feel of turning its clear fluted stem must've been the feeling Harlan had when she thought she possessed me.

"Marry me," she said.

My laughter rained down.

"A ring, at least. At least a ceremony."

We stood, glass between us, law outside us, two women raining. The clock ticked the hour and I knew time was up. Glancing around, I realized that she'd rearranged the furniture in the apartment we shared. Every piece butted up against another. The whole apartment was a giant corner.

I felt like tide when it has nowhere to go but sharks. I could see thousands of glinty edges grabbing at my skirt like teeth.

"Will you give her up?"

Why can't a woman love more than one mover? Why must she choose, why must she split herself in two? I loved Harlan with the soft sweet love that my fingers, lips, and breasts were made of; I loved water with the fierce bold passion that kept my heart beating and my muscles taut. Together my loves built my body; together they shaped me. They let me breathe and swallow both.

A few nights later we drove to the pool.

Midnight. A Saturday. We startled the janitor. "Night lessons," I said. He frowned but let me use my key. Harlan and I stole into the desperate water. Standing side-by-side, our clothes plastered to our ribs and thighs, we kissed and tousled each other's hair. Through so much wet, through so much weight, she slipped one finger between my lips and I felt my legs tug her inside.

"Say good-bye," she said.

How could I choose otherwise? Take a finger or a lover. My body spoke. Her inner gravity was too much for me, though I didn't come, but doubled over.

Only after she was dry on shore, rubbing her hair with a towel, did I let water enter me for the last time.

Her hands not separate from my self, but of it.

Her motion not outside my skin, but from it.

Water met wet. One slickness. One shiver. Shaking in the shallows I realized my mistake.

But I keep the promises I make.

Climbing out of the pool, I trailed my left hand across the mirrored surface. Since then, my fingers tingle when I'm heartlost.

It was a cruel good-bye.

If blue rose up, I didn't see it. I'd turned my back on all wet things.

Dryness my ring. My ring to Harlan.

Water was the other woman.

WATER : DRIZZLE

When she realized my unhappiness, years after my promise, Harlan tried to ease my ache. This time, instead of banishing what I most longed for, she tried becoming my beloved element.

Not substitute or simulacrum. The undulating thing itself.

At first I believed silk sheets could be liquid. Believed a flickering candle shone the same as foam. And her fingers within me, gentle and tidal. And her hips rocking my hips, her lips moistening mine. I let her think I'd come when she rested her head on my breasts and squirmed and sighed. But there's more to a flip than proximity and pressure.

Inside water is more water.

Water permeates, becoming part of its lover. As it entered me, we were already one.

The thing I most want is the thing I most fear.

To lose myself, becoming part of something bigger.

There can be no good-bye to what's most of your body.

What I said *good-bye* to wasn't water.

What I said *good-bye* to was desire.

Thirst. I learned to see and not want. I learned to think of water as a necessity. I learned to make it part of me without pleasure, without tremor, without whispering its name or feeling its softness.

Blue . . .

I promised.

Blue . . .

I promised Harlan.

She says I talk in my sleep.
I think I swim.

Begin at the beginning is poor advice for an element. Water circles, and wind, and the sun's hot violet. Once I had a student who could understand waves.

And the one who filled her, weighing her down with stones — slowly, slowly, till her shy heart sank? He folded the paper and dipped his spoon in sweet cereal. He spoke his wife's name like he was drunk at a funeral.

The girl, my student, did the thing the lost do, desperate. She whispered his name to a shifting element. Maybe she wanted the whole thing erased — his name, his stones, her belly. Memory. But the bay clung to her words, letters for its court of law.

She was a girl, a little sweaty, shaped like licorice, gawky, giggly.

Why would a man ride a girl's sleepy body?

Amateur athletes think of motion as struggle and chase. But the keen ones, the stars, fall in love with their elements. A great runner's feet caress the track, becoming speed and then earth; a prima's ribs rise, becoming breathing and then air; an Olympic-bound swimmer's arms stroke water, indistinguishable from her element, indistinguishable from need.

I watch water, not my students' bodies. The crimped blue surface tells me where they've been.

But Rose — a decade back. Rose Hobble. I remember something swam within her. When she passed me in the hall, I thought of flesh and sinew. She'd quit the team late junior year — a sore shoulder — but stayed away so long I didn't believe her.

Sores split and blossom, but also heal. Rose's sore was a longing, a slow rise and call.

I don't love bodies, but the elements that make them. I don't like thinking of the subtleties of procreation. But she stood a Madonna in the lunch line at noon. I watched her fill her tray with milk. I watched her eat all by herself.

Only water has ever flipped me.

From the start it was deeper, because water was here. When we kissed, I was already wet; when I came, I bled forth what had founded desire. I was of the water, though I loved it more — more than myself or any sweet *Her.*

I can't remember not knowing the feeling of blue.

At three I was paddling. At seven, competing. And before three, before seven, before birth was swimming.

Harlan's forgotten what a child's body knows. But the pull to love's as strong as the pull to memory.

I live in an apartment two flights up from Harlan's. Mornings, I listen for the mewl of her door. The central staircase is a periscope. Sometimes I'm an eye pressed against cool glass; sometimes all I see is water. Sometimes I wish I were her next-door neighbor.

In the years after our split I used the rails for perspective. The point of the *V* held each face like a lens.

Like all works of genius, coaching happened by accident. I came to renown because I followed desire. Not many girls could adapt to my method. I asked them to dance and to spy and to sing. I favored sleepswimmers. Ghost girls who whispered. My technique was stealth: not disturbing the blue.

Every year, I started with fifteen swimmers. By October I had four or five. My pool was magic. The lanes knew their names. Water singled them out, judging dives, sprints, and strokes. The girls who handled water roughly — breaking the surface, kicking attack — still seemed surprised when water fought back.

It rose up and over them.

It stifled and coughed them.

They sat on the sidelines, choking its name.

The best coaches read their swimmers by watching water's geometry.

Soon I owned an umbrella.

My own moisture dried up.

I've tried. I've stayed away from water. If I pace the pool every day, what's that? I don't dunk. I don't splash. I don't dip my toes. When the girls dive in, I step two feet back.

I watch them swim. I know the feeling. I remember my chest seeking the pulse of her blood.

Water won't take me back. If I left, I'd be solo.

Without water. Without Harlan.

I made a promise.

I also made the wrong decision.

But so what? That's love. That's the story of religion. That's marriage and war. All human life is suffering. Who am I to believe I should be the rare blissy high one?

To be a teacher is to pass along hope you don't have.

To watch others dive. To live through their flutterings.

I gave Violet a test. Two laps each: butterfly, freestyle, breast.

I knew after the first. And I stood staring, not at her strokes, not at blue spume, but at time made visible.

What I gave up.

What I could give her.

What I could teach a young lover of water.

Violet's eyes were the only thing I saw. Her body — still — I don't remember. There was water; where water wasn't, that was Violet. That slicked out space. No arms, no legs, no breasts, no belly. But her eyes — even while she lapped it, I could see to her soul.

She was the negative; water, the photo.

Small slits broadened when she rose out of the blue.

Those scars didn't heal. The surface stayed raw.

Violet brought shipwrecks with her. Loch Ness her familiar.

She had a look I recognized while she was in the water. I'd call it hunger but it was more than that. More than hunger, because there's a deeper level. Not *desire,* not *need,* but the overlap of the two.

She'd stare across the pool like she was stretched over a woman's body. She'd reach too far and grab. It wasn't polite, the thing she wanted. The thing she wanted was the pool — to be of it, not just swimming. To be part of the thing the other swimmers fought. They'd chop, they'd cut, they'd carve space for themselves. I could see their bodies. Violet blended in.

They wanted out, she wanted in.

The water knew it. Responded to her as it had to me. Closed in around her instead of backing off. Her times were amazing because she wasn't fighting.

Poor Rose Hobble. I saw her rising belly glow. Offered my hand, but she spit in the water. And her skin glowed bolder. And an absence hung around her shoulders.

How can a girl believe in her body if she's taught not to believe her voice?

Rose was invisible. She drowned in the classroom before she hit the water. And some go on teaching that way, telling the same story — *this is reality, this is what's true.*

Gaslighting the girls.

How many fall through?

Two years later, I gave her money in an envelope. And rain.

They found the first under the second. She never used it.

I know his name.

He's important; he's official. He drives around town in a coal-colored Beemer.

It's too late to save her.

But the daughter . . .

The night Rose drowned I broke one of my rules. I went walking in grey drizzly weather, out into the rain, thinking lightning would strike me. I waited for fire to dry my best blue. Instead wetness surrounded me. Water was where I wasn't. I waited so long I became part of the storm.

Across town, over pipes, under rain's shifting awning, the space between drops outlined girls' shivering gowns. The prom rolled on, its own red carpet.

Rose dropped to her knees. No stopping it.

At first I thought I was hearing tide scritch. Over and over, like gravel on sand. Over and over, a dull repetition. Then the syllables formed; then I had my first vision.

I dreamed I saw him sailing. Water spread violent colors, surrounding the boat, scarlet letters of sun-flecked foam.

I want to stand on the banks of the bay and see justice in the white-capped waves and terrible salt. I want to say that water remembers the name Rose whispered. I want to say it cared enough for her body, for her ghost, that when The Big Man's boat sailed past Lummi Island, a swell stirred from beneath the crust, blue rose up, The Big Man drowned. I want to say he suffered, repented, was forgiven. I want to say his death was the sacrifice needed to transform the world from a place where women are broken to a place where love is wanted and born. I want to say that, once he was gone, Rose rose from the dead. That her daughter was hers again. I want to say she and Violet lived happily ever after, in a cabin by the water, with three cats and a great window.

I want to tell stories and believe they'll come true. But the dead are dead, and the living continue.

He has a wife and two daughters. He has a house on the hill. I've seen him now and again, drinking beer at a brewpub, cutting his meat, knife tight in his hand.

His eyes are very blue, the color of the bay at noon.

He probably doesn't remember Rose's name.

The things water holds! That's why I love it. When I bend my ear to the surface, the secrets it spumes! But it's a burden, knowing, as it was a burden for Rose. That's why she spat his name into the ocean, hoping that gesture would clean her mouth.

Who's dirty, then?

She trusted the bay to save what she birthed him.

She was my student. I tended to her knowledge like it had its own heart. I taught her specifics — freestyle, back, fly. I taught her speed; I taught her stillness. I taught her the secret of the wait before the gun.

In teaching her waiting, did I teach her too much? What could I have shown her that would have saved her?

WATER : DRIZZLE

Should I have taught her anger; should I have taught her fear?

Nothing you give a student is enough. You can only prepare them for that one small thing — the circle you've drawn in chaos.

Discipline.

The moment of spark meeting thought, the fine line, where to stop.

Glitter

I have a simple answer to complex questions about creation — *art must be a sponge.* What is vital for the life of any writing project is that it be flexible enough to absorb all daily spill-over. When a writer finds characters, ideas, sounds, or even a plot flexible enough to incorporate quotidian happenings, writing becomes, not just pleasurable, but spiritual. Writing becomes a way to stave off loss and to stay sane.

No matter what I am writing, I need a project thick and dense enough to absorb everything that happens to me. If someone close to me is hurt or blessed, if I discover new parts of myself, if I inherit a shirt with spangled parrots on the sleeves, I want to be able to incorporate those things immediately into my work. My daily morning writing practice is about translating whatever feels pressing into the language of the project I'm working on.

A good project allows me to absorb both big and small occurrences, to combine and blend them until my life is indistinguishable from history, fantasy, magic, music. As a sponge absorbs liquid until the liquid becomes the sponge, the original pieces become the project; ultimately they should be indistinguishable from it.

When something in a text stands out significantly, usually this means that the writer emphasized some autobiographical detail too heavily. I tell my students that such stand-outs, important as they might be to the writer's heart, may need to be cut from the piece, or at least absorbed more completely. My friend John Clower calls this "Killing your babies." Often the "babies" a writer must kill are the seeds of the original project. Once a project is underway, it should become self-sustaining. As this happens, the writer needs to give it autonomy, allowing her or his wants to become secondary.

Fat Rosie wouldn't let me incorporate things. I was frustrated writing it, because when something interesting (or even banal) happened, I couldn't find ways of incorporating it into the text. The writing style was so taut and cautious that incorporating much of anything was a problem. While this is often true for poems, writing a poem does not demand the kind of time commitment required of a novel. A poem is a date; a novel is a marriage. Short stories fall somewhere in-between, which is probably why so few lesbians are interested in them.

I do not believe in writer's block — the idea that a writer can simply sit and stare and think of nothing interesting for longer than, say, ten minutes. I don't understand imaginations that shut off. What I do understand is stammering — grasping for a new alphabet, longing for new sounds to better express the hazy meaning of the passing scenery. We view life from a speeding car; we're dogs, poking awkward snouts past glass. Everything whizzes, too fast to keep up. Even once we understand something kinesthetically or emotionally, our minds may struggle to find the language to express it. I do not believe in writer's block, but in the slippage between experience and alphabet.

When I moved to Bellingham, my cat Addy was killed by a coyote. If I had been writing another kind of novel when this happened, my grief would have been unconsciously sopped up by the text. When I sat down to write the next day, I would have been preoccupied with loss. Thinking about loss, I would have been inclined to write loss into one of the character's lives. Someone would have lost a child. Or lost their home to an earthquake. Or lost their wallet. Someone would have lost their name to amnesia or their grandmother to Alzheimer's. Conversely, longing for Addy's return, I might have depicted the reunion of two long-estranged characters, or a simple description — an old rowboat overgrown with weeds

— that reminded me of Addy, but that my readers would associate with a retired fisherman's front yard.

I did incorporate Addy into *Fat Rosie and Rose*, but it felt like a digression rather than an organic character development. It felt tacked-on in a way that the missionaries in my novel *Switch* or Maureen's mother in *Seeing Dell* did not, even though those characters were absorbed late in the writing from real life. *Fat Rosie* sometimes acted like a stubborn two-year old, bawling. It balked and balked, refusing to let any additions get close, yet not generating enough material from within to become autonomous.

If a piece resists autobiographical material, this may be because it is begging you to stop imposing your life on it — trying to move from within, to take unexpected turns that the characters, and not you, want to take. But this wasn't the case with *Fat Rosie*, either. Those two ways of moving forward — autobiographical additions and organic development — are the most conventional. There is a third, sound, and a fourth, image. And ultimately that was how the novel moved forward — through sensory associations, puns and rhythm, gesture and color. But those connections weren't strong enough, in this instance, to sustain the flow. That was a great disappointment to me, for at one point I'd hoped that *Fat Rosie* would function like some of Gertrude Stein's great work, or like Carole Maso's *Aureole*, in which fragments come to sound like lovers speaking of passion, loss, desire, and intuition. But I couldn't pull it off. The novel functioned neither as realism, nor pastiche; neither as a conventional conflict, crisis, resolution plot, nor as accretion. This shames me; this is the failure for which I blame myself, which most reflects, not some difficult outside circumstance, but my own artistic limitations.

I'd never had this problem with fiction before. When I wrote my first novel, after about a year of writing short fiction, I remember feeling that I'd discovered a new continent, so wide and expansive did the genre seem. I love writing novels precisely because anything can be tossed in. So for someone who is very prolific, for whom pages and pages can flow in a matter of hours, the experience of sitting in front of my computer day after day, month after month, and getting maybe six bad lines in a week was unbelievably discouraging. When I am writing poetry I might be happy with six lines — might be ecstatic, might consider it a poem — but this was different, because the lines felt like stammering, like I'd lost my writing self rather than found a new, concise Carol. It made me want to stop writing, but obviously I didn't. Unfinished, *Fat Rosie* would have hovered, ghost-like, above the keyboard. I had to finish it, even knowing full well it was going to fail. And *Fat Rosie and Rose* is, to my mind, a failure. I don't say this lightly; I wouldn't say it of my previous books, published or unpublished. Whatever their flaws (and there are many), they succeed at enough things to satisfy me. But *Fat Rosie* never made me happy. The honeymoon never happened; the struggle stage — of development, meandering, anxiety, constant revision — just went on and on, until it gradually became clear to me that this book was it: my first huge mistake, a Rorschach blotty beyond meaning.

For one, it is not Rose's story, which is what I wanted it to be. I wanted to get inside her head, describe her in such a way that, by the time she murdered her infant (the original climax of the novel), the reader understood why, and empathized with her. I wanted to force my readers to feel her panic and desperation, to feel the necessity, to her, of her action. But I failed. And when I shifted the focus of the text to the love triangle (during the stage when I called the book *Ghostwater*), I failed again.

I tell my students that to be ambitious means to try and fail — that there is no such thing as "finding your voice." That phrase irritates me; like "writer's block," it belies the complexity of writers' processes. Both are phrases useful to academics who teach workshops, but not to the writer struggling at the computer. "Finding your voice," like "coming out," is a poor metaphor because it implies that the thing need only happen once. What then to make of the accomplished writer who has hit her stride in several books, only to suddenly find herself stammering?

A writer who does the same thing over and over may have a recognizable voice, but I would not call her an artist. Artists challenge themselves and push the boundaries of their art by taking risks; risk-taking guarantees both growth and failure. It also demands periods of slug-gish productivity while the artist struggles to find new ways to express new thoughts and feelings. I tell my stu-dents that I would rather see a messy, incomplete piece full of genuine emotion and insight than a polished, structurally sound story that is one long cliche. But it's one thing to tell students something, and another thing to tell yourself.

Fat Rosie had and has such emotional significance that I couldn't just jettison it. While the book failed to work for me as a coherent whole, its crazy shape seemed to be a sign that I was ready to break new ground as an artist. For example, in *Fat Rosie* I blurred the line between poetry and prose more often, and oddly, than I'd ever done before. Poets use line breaks like an additional form of punctuation; fiction writers should be able to do something similar. In *Fat Rosie* I tried to, occasionally breaking sentences as in a poem, but more often breaking paragraphs with the same at-tention to sound and tempo that a poet brings to line breaks. This attention to sound extended to the syntax and rhythm of each line. Portions of the novel were writ-ten to a sort of metronome that whirred in my head when I sat down to write.

Late in the summer of 1998 I decided to write a pref-ace explaining how the novel was evolving — from a book focusing on Rose's act of infanticide to a book fo-cusing on Violet's love affair with Rose. The preface also promised to give me space to discuss the political issues which fueled my work. If the novel failed, at least the preface would encourage readers to think about the topic, and about the process of writing in general.

What happened next felt like what happened when Violet's voice and the love triangle plot supplanted Rose's voice and story. Suddenly the preface interested me more and more; it grew from three pages describing the novel's origins to twenty describing my feelings about abortion and maternity. Shortly thereafter, I put the novel aside and began pounding out a long, detailed explanation of why I was writing it — even as I wasn't.

In October I wrote "Red," an essay separate from the mess I was making of *Fat Rosie*, a mess now part autobiography, part fiction, part sermon. But once "Red" was written, I couldn't help but see the connections — couldn't help but feel that in "Red" I'd done a better job of capturing some of what I'd set out to depict in the novel. I began trying to come up with ways to connect "Red" to *Fat Rosie*; adding it to the preface seemed the most obvious solution. Not long after, it occurred to me to call the preface (which ultimately would not make it into the final draft of *Gaslight*) "White." Once I had "White" and "Red" side-by-side, I began making notes for a few other pieces. Following "Red" and "White" came "Rose," "Blue," and "Silver." Organizing the book by color freed me up; the dreadful mess — the drudgery — of *Fat Rosie* was transformed into a lively project, something I craved time to work on. Maybe there is an inevitability to structure that gives a false but pleasant sense of inevitability to content. At any rate, with the idea of using colors to structure the chapters, what had been the preface to the book became the book itself.

What then to do with *Fat Rosie*? It seemed a sad trick to play on my readers to continually make reference to a book as if the book were some Bible or other, and then insert it, say, at the end of the memoir, only to have the readers discover that what preceded the novel, the novel's explanation, was more interesting than the referenced text. But it didn't occur to me to jettison the novel; I felt (and obviously still feel) that I could make something of its failure, make its failure into an example, use it to fuel an analysis of my process and aesthetic. The original preface to *Fat Rosie* had incorporated some attempts to analyze the weird shape of the book — thoughts on the way the circumstances of my life caused the book's fragmented structure. I wanted to expand that, to ask questions about how and why I write fiction. And so I decided to start writing about *Fat Rosie*'s production, and see where my words took me.

Gaslight is a book about writing a novel that does not exist.

Yet that statement — funky and postmodern as it sounds — is another lie, another fiction. I did write *Fat Rosie and Rose*; it does exist. But it's a mess, and might well sit in a drawer until I die and it gets recycled. I had to let go of trying to make *Fat Rosie* the center of the book and allow the book to realign itself. The new structure was color; the new center, uncomfortable as I might be with it, was my life. From the realization that I needed to relegate what had once been the entire project — the novel — to a footnote of the new text came yet another rush of freedom, the freedom of following the trajectory a book will take once the author steps out of its way.

I can't say why autobiography is working as a sponge for me right now. That's the mystery of art — what you're ready for as an artist, and when, and why. I've made *Fat Rosie* part of *Gaslight* because I feel it will intrigue readers invested in the process of writing, in the evolution of an artist's style, in the particular stresses placed on women and queer writers, and in the relation, for one writer, between teaching, writing, and life. I wish that more writers showed the muddy footprints leading to the doorstep. Process matters to me; it is the best part, the mystery. I don't feel that baring the skeleton of one's process is indecent; it doesn't damage the spiritual element of writing, the prayer and the rush. There is an element of the creative process that will always be a great gasp — craziness, inexplicable. The trance state I enter when I create is not damaged by discussing creation. What damages it is feeling silenced — whether by sexism, homophobia, violence, or simply an inattentive audience.

The fragments I've included here from *Fat Rosie and Rose* are not simple, but what writing is? I find it odd that my students assume realism — with its coincidences, precise detail, and carefully-wrought plots — is easier to understand than *sound*. *Fat Rosie* is about sound — the sound a woman makes when she has had enough.

And hope. The ending surprised me — I, who am so pessimistic, so angry, so afraid. I wrote the ending in a daze, healed by Violet's encounter with a young girl, an encounter I wanted the reader to understand would function as the beginning of the young girl's new life — her ability to speak, to swim to shore.

As I envisioned it, ten years after Rose's death Violet would work for Coach helping with a girl's swim team at the Y. And one day a ten year old girl would walk into the sunlit space of the pool — into the shimmer. She'd shine; she'd glitter in water, blue and gold; she'd look so much like Rose. And the reader would understand that she was Rose's girl, the child Rose did not kill in the complex moments after giving birth, before drowning herself.

The novel came full circle. Rose did not commit infanticide, but left her child behind, on sand. Violet saved her. And this girl became, not Rose or Violet or Coach, but a new one, different, stronger, less damaged — a girl to save the ones who'd come after. A lifeguard, a muse, Shakespeare's sister. She would straddle sand and water, old and new, loving women and men, learning and teaching. She would be a kind of saint, only not a martyr.

St. Pleasure, this girl would be.

Violet would see.

I walk alone, often, by the bay. I'm not waiting for Rose anymore, but trying to say good-bye. To her ghost, yes, but to my ghost, too. To the girl who believed that the right flip would save her.

The water whispers.

I know his name at last.

When I heard it the first time I thought about *fire*. I thought about buying a gun and retrieving what he took from her.

But there's the daughter.

Ten, she is.

A few weeks ago I got a call from my old coach. She's still at Whatcom High, where Rose and I used to swim. She wanted to know did I want to help — Saturdays at the Y, where she coaches a girl's team.

I had to think it over. An hour later I called her back.

"How old are they?" I asked.

But I already knew.

✧

I took their hands and led them past the blue mirror. We were swimmers together.

Coach waded in, too.

And the surprise of that — Coach knee-high in blue — helped me forget.

About Rose, about Harlan.
How they're both gone.

✧

Five minutes later the last girl rushed in — speeding, her face streaming *sorry.* And her body.

I thought *this changes everything.*

She looked like Rose.

Coach already knew.

At first I felt sick. I turned away, tried to pretend I hadn't seen. But she scuffed her sandals beside me, unshy, wanting in, wanting to learn what her body could do.

I bit my lip and made myself look. I said, "Speed makes good swimmers," and asked her to join the others.

✧

She swam like Rose.

The same motion.

Brazen.

✧

After, I patted her shoulders with a towel. I said, "You're such a fine swimmer." I said, "I can't believe you braved the breakers." She beamed, her lips blue.

I said "Your mother was a swimmer too."

Blue

First the *V* of the flocks, then frost on the moorings. Threads of snow, not enough for a sheet. And you, waiting. Far from me. Holding. And me, longing for the creak-snap of your heart's blue ice.

At dusk I pace circles around the bay, black prints on black gravel, my movement redundant. In triangles on the grass above the stippled rocks, geese sleep standing up. Each tucks one leg to its breast; all but the lookout tucks its head to its wings.

The lookout stares forward.

You glance back. And begin.

There is a return that is more than *turn back.* There is a return that moves forward even as it honors memory. At dusk the bay smooths to a sheet. I could spread it wide, indigo stretched cerulean. Wide enough for two-turned-one.

Return to me, though we cannot marry. Though we are not citizens — never *safe,* never *equal.* Return is tidal. Tidal, meaning *pull.* Tuck your ice to my breast. Home, meaning *yes.*

We will live here as lookouts, tossing crackers to the greedy gulls. Card-carrying lesbians. Press my pun to your lips; I am writing to you.

We of the hunted flock. We who have become migration, our maps made of intuition. Blue girls flying through the afterglow.

In the shadow of the tall laws our wings spread wide enough indeed.

Fawn

In the lush, generous landscape where I live now, I am finding something liminal in tint, temperature, and echo. I see my own spiritual concerns mirrored in the steel-blue bay and violet mountains. Perhaps this is the ugliest human quality of all — imposing our world view on the wilderness around us. Nonetheless, in the absence of faith in some god, in the absence of belief in the lies about love and family that heterosexual culture taught me, I find it necessary to look beyond humans for solace. Lately, I have stolen that solace from a neighbor, a neighbor I wish I could speak with.

She comes out early in the morning when the grass is still wet. Often I see her as I round the corner of my house, my dog nipping my heels as Corgis do to show loyalty or jealousy. She comes and I follow. When I let

Ely out at six, the doe is sitting in the weeds beside the shed, legs folded into origami. She turns her head slowly; when Ely's ears twitch, she snorts and unfolds. There's a moment of stillness before Ely yaps and the doe struts into the brush, her steps strangely awkward, nothing like silk. In the stillness I think of what comes next: the walk to the weeds, bending down, kissing damp earth. In the stillness I taste her breath and feel her color, the color of gravity, the tender fawn that leads her back to brush.

Sometimes she sits like she's reading a letter. Sometimes she sits like she's listening for cougar. Sometimes she just sits and I think that she's like me, trapped between the highway and the woods. I don't know many things about the doe but I understand liminality, its beauty and danger. I feel a kinship with her, with her curiosity, with her susceptibility to the lure of both the ubiquitous and the wilderness.

The highway passes me by beyond my fence. I can see the blur of cars, color and speed, but no faces. And travelers can see even less of where I'm standing; I know because I've driven past, craning my neck to see, seeing nothing. So I tug up the blinds and watch time, watch the doe graze, watch the road cut through the tree wall. I watch and I wait, because I want to learn patience.

My house could be part of the forest, with its mossy roof and restless yard, or part of the freeway, with its electric lights and noisy clatter. The dumb sweet drift of DJs blends with the rush of traffic till it's all white noise. Ely shivers, chasing the doe in her twitchy-eyed sleep.

WATER : FAWN

Outside it's blue and several greens at once. The wilderness keeps coming, hoping to push the freeway back.

Back, where it came from. Back to humans who snaked its circles through another home, a village really, really a city, where the doe lived, and coyote, and cougar, and animals smaller, maybe larger too. The doe lives where she does because the highway circled round, turning woods and farmland into a small coiled cove of refuge between its asphalt bumblings and pastel suburbia. The doe lives where she does because the highway's cut her off forever from the far and wide she used to know.

Sometimes I wake from dreaming *forever* and know that I was cut off from home, too. But the home I imagine is not a place, but a person; not any person, but a woman, a woman much like myself, a woman who is, perhaps, myself in another incarnation, ripe with freedom and its possibilities. I wait for her, because I understand refuge and I understand anger. Like the cougar, who've started jumping humans, seeing old predators as prey. The great cat drops from its tree — for we can never own them — and circles its victim's neck with claws like an embrace. They do the strangle, a wild dance. The cougar gouges and blood goes and the dance turns from a circle to a stomp to a pile on the ground.

We're closing in. How can we blame them if they pounce their attacks?

CAROL GUESS *GASLIGHT* 187

I watch the doe negotiate her weedy gaza, avoiding the cold pulse of the highway to her left, the feeble glimmer of coffee lights and neon to her right. I try with my silence to tell her I too am trapped. In the gauzy light of early morning, her meditations seem like witnessing. *Join me,* she says, *follow the in-between.*

Where the sound of breath becomes important.

I want gauzy light and animals that teach me; I want the woman I'm waiting for, the one I could be, to make her own damped-down circle visible. When I stumble back onto the porch, I want the in-between to follow me inside.

About the author

Carol Guess is the author of two novels, **Seeing Dell** and **Switch**. She teaches GLBT literature and creative writing at Western Washington University, and lives in Seattle.

other fine lesbian books from

Odd Girls Press
P. O. Box 2157, Anaheim CA 92814-0157
800-821-0632 email: publisher@oddgirlspress.com
web: www.oddgirlspress.com

Monologues and Scenes for Lesbian Actors by Carolyn Gage. Finally! A book for lesbians who are tired of "passing" at auditions and in acting classes and workshops! Here at last, from one of the most talented and inventive contemporary playwrights, is a book of twenty-five monologues and forty-five scenes by, for, and about lesbians. 1-887237-10-0 $15.95 trade paper.

Pelt by Daphne Gottlieb. Using the language of the everyday to express the extraordinary, poet Daphne Gottlieb searches for the truths of human experience and finds those truths in relationships, childhood, and a woman on fire. From preying to praying, the loss of innocence and the innocence of loss, and the most cruel and unusual stuff of all — love — these poems represent a strong, fresh voice in contemporary poetry. 1-887237-09-7 $9 trade paper.

Gaslight by Carol Guess. Carol Guess has composed, from glass-edged fragments of her life and her work as a creative artist, the mosaic of a woman who has fought to be her true self. Her adversaries have been many, and formidable. Those who dictated the ideal shape of her female body and the correct dimensions of her sexuality as she emerged from a childhood in the south, ensnared in sexual exploitation and a spiral of anorexia. The teachers who attempted to extinguish her ambition and identity as a creative artist—because female writing could not possibly rise above the trivial. The politics of art and sexuality that continue to litter her path as a lesbian academic and a serious artist. *Gaslight* speaks to the expressive individual you have struggled to become. To the questing child and adolescent you once were. Like no other book, *Gaslight* shares each step of the interior process of creation and of failing to create: the process of becoming a writer. In this extraordinary and unforgettable work, Carol Guess brilliantly illuminates the path to art and to individuality. 1-887237-05-4 $15.99 trade paper

First Resort by Nanci Little. Jordan Bryant maintains an almost clinical distance between herself and the people she meets at Catawamteak, the grand resort on the coast of Maine where she is Director of Golf . . . until she meets Gillian Benson. *First Resort i*s a meticulous exploration of the growth of the bonds of affection, love, & friendship between women.1-887237-01-1 $11 trade paper.

Night Mare by Franci McMahon. Jane Scott has been investigating a cruel scandal in her world, the theft and/or killing of prized horses for their insurance value. When she accompanies her best friend to evaluate an Arabian horse, Jane knows its price is too cheap — way too cheap. Suddenly, shockingly, Jane is embroiled in a devastating murder — for which she blames herself. A murder that hurls her into the orbit of a beautiful, wild-spirited mare named Night. A murder that will take her to Montana, and to the ranch of a singular woman who holds the power to penetrate every border of Jane's well-guarded, grieving self. 1-887237-14-3 $13 trade paper

Bloodsong by Karen Marie Christa Minns. In lyric and erotic prose, Minns continues the story of the vampire Darsen, first introduced in her Lammy-nominated **Virago**. Against her will, Ginny has been given the bite that is transforming her into a vampire. As Darsen waits for her victim to weaken, Ginny's lover Manilla readies herself for the confrontation when Darsen returns to claim Ginny forever. 1-887237-08-9 $12.95 trade paper.

Tory's Tuesday by Linda Kay Silva. Captured by Nazis while trying to flee Poland, Marissa and Elsa are shipped to the Auschwitz concentration camp, where they are separated. Through the atrocities and horrors both women face, their love for each other never wavers. They meet other courageous women who help them in their fight to survive and reunite. 1-887237-06-2 trade paper.

ORDERING Our books are available at feminist bookstores, gay and lesbian bookstores, and some independent bookstores and mail-order services. If the book you are looking for is not in stock, the store will order it for you. To order directly from Odd Girls Press please send a list of titles you want and a check for the total + $3.00 to cover shipping charges (Canada $5.00, all other countries 15% of the total cost of books being ordered)

SUBMISSIONS We're always looking for new works. For submission guidelines send a self-addressed stamped envelope to Odd Girls Press or go to our web site and see the Submissions Guidelines web page.